DTF Printers User Guide

Maintenance and Troubleshooting of DTF Transfer
Film, Powder, Ink, Prints, Printers, and Everything
About DTF Printing

By

Elena Brook

Contents

Introduction

Stepping into the world of Direct-to-Film (DTF) printing was like unlocking a new realm of possibilities. I remember the first time I encountered DTF technology- it was at a printing press show, and the vibrant colours and sharp details of the prints captivated me immediately. As a seasoned graphic designer and print enthusiast, I thought I had seen it all with screen printing and sublimation. But DTF offered something different, something more versatile and efficient. I was hooked.

Embarking on this journey with DTF printing has been an exhilarating ride filled with both challenges and triumphs. My initial foray into DTF wasn't without its hiccups. Setting up the printer for the first time was a maze of cables and calibration, and navigating the intricacies of RIP software felt like learning a new language. Yet, each hurdle I overcame was a step closer to mastering this transformative printing method.

The allure of DTF printing is undeniable. Imagine the ability to transfer any design, in all its colourful glory, onto virtually any fabric or material. No need for pre-treatment, and no limitations on fabric type or colour. It's the ultimate tool for customization, whether you're printing intricate artwork on a t-shirt or creating personalized bags, hats, and even shoes.

As I delved deeper into the DTF process, I realized the immense potential it held for both small businesses and large-scale production. The flexibility and efficiency it offers are unparalleled. With DTF, I could easily produce short runs without the setup costs and time constraints typical of traditional methods. The quality was consistently impressive, with vibrant colours and durable finishes that stood up to repeated wear and washing.

But with great potential came the need for great precision. I soon learned that achieving those flawless prints required a keen eye for detail and a thorough understanding of the technology. From aligning the film perfectly to selecting the right print settings and profiles, every step mattered. And let's not forget the crucial stages of curing, heat pressing, and cooling, which can make or break the final product.

Maintaining the printer and troubleshooting issues became part of my routine, each task bringing a deeper appreciation for the machinery and the process. Regular cleaning, careful handling of film, and managing ink levels were not just chores but essential practices that ensured my printer remained in peak condition, delivering top-notch results time and again.

Through trial and error, and countless hours of experimentation, I honed my skills and built a robust workflow. The rewards were worth it – seeing my designs come to life with such clarity and vibrancy was incredibly satisfying. And the response from clients? Nothing short of enthusiastic. They loved the quality and durability of DTF prints, which opened new avenues for creativity and Business growth.

In writing this guide to DTF printing and mastering direct-to-film technology, I wanted to share the knowledge and insights I gained through my experiences. This guide is more than a technical manual; it's a companion for anyone eager to explore and excel in DTF printing. Whether you're just starting out or looking to refine your skills, this book is designed to help you navigate the complexities of DTF technology and unlock its full potential.

Together, we'll delve into the nitty-gritty of printer setup, design preparation, and print execution. We'll tackle the intricacies of RIP software and colour management, and I'll walk you through each step of the process with clear, practical advice. You'll learn how to troubleshoot common issues, maintain your equipment, and create stunning prints that stand out in the marketplace.

Join me on this journey into the vibrant, versatile world of DTF printing. Let's transform your creative ideas into brilliant, lasting works of art. Welcome to this ultimate guide to DTF Printing. Let's make magic happen!

What is DTF Printing?

Direct-to-film (DTF) printing is a modern and versatile digital printing technique that involves printing designs directly onto a special transfer film. This method is particularly popular in the custom apparel industry due to its flexibility and high-quality results.

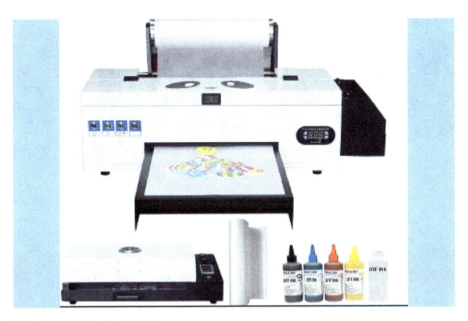

How DTF Printing Works:

1. **Design Creation:** The process begins with creating or selecting a digital design using graphic design software.
2. **Printing on Film:** The design is printed onto a specialized PET film using a DTF printer. Unlike traditional inkjet printing, DTF uses a combination of textile ink and adhesive powder.
3. **Powder Application:** A special adhesive powder is applied to the printed film while the ink is still wet. This powder ensures the design adheres to the fabric.
4. **Curing:** The film with the applied powder is then cured in a curing oven or using a heat press to solidify the adhesive layer.
5. **Transfer:** The cured film is placed onto the desired fabric, and the design is transferred using a heat press, which activates the adhesive to bond the design to the fabric.
6. **Peeling:** After cooling, the PET film is peeled away, leaving the design affixed to the fabric.

Key Components in DTF Printing:

- **DTF Printer:** A specialized printer equipped to handle the unique requirements of DTF printing, including handling textile inks.

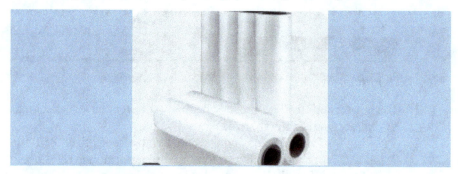

- **PET Film:** A special film that can withstand the heat and pressure of the transfer process and provides a base for the design.

- **Textile Ink:** Pigment-based inks are designed to adhere to the PET film and provide vibrant, long-lasting prints.

- **Adhesive Powder:** A crucial element that ensures the ink sticks to the fabric during the transfer process.

- **Curing Equipment:** Devices like a heat press or curing oven that solidify the adhesive powder on the film.

Key Features and Benefits of DTF Printing

DTF printing has revolutionized the custom printing industry by offering several advantages over traditional methods such as screen printing and Direct-to-Garment (DTG) printing.

Versatility:

- DTF printing works on a wide range of fabrics, including cotton, polyester, blends, and even non-textile materials like wood and leather.
- It supports detailed and intricate designs, including full-colour images and gradients, without the limitations of screen printing.

High-Quality Results:

- DTF prints produce bright and vivid colours, making them ideal for colourful designs and photographs.
- The prints are durable, with good washability and resistance to cracking and fading.

Efficiency and Cost-Effectiveness:

- Unlike screen printing, DTF printing does not require costly screens or plates, making it cost-effective for small runs and custom orders.
- The process is relatively fast, allowing for quick production times and same-day printing for urgent orders.

Customization and Personalization:

- DTF is perfect for producing short runs or even single pieces, catering to the growing demand for personalized products.
- Easily incorporate unique data (e.g., names, numbers) into each print, ideal for customized apparel like sports jerseys or promotional items.

Applications of DTF Printing

DTF printing's versatility and quality make it suitable for a broad range of applications across various industries.

- **Custom T-Shirts:** Perfect for producing custom t-shirts with detailed designs and vivid colours.
- **Sportswear:** Ideal for printing names, numbers, and logos on jerseys and athletic wear.
- **Fashion Accessories:** Used for creating unique designs on caps, bags, and other accessories.
- **Corporate Merchandise:** Producing branded merchandise like tote bags, caps, and promotional apparel.
- **Event Souvenirs:** Custom prints for events, such as concerts, festivals, and trade shows.
- **Custom Textiles:** Printing on home textiles such as cushions, tablecloths, and curtains.
- **Art and Crafts:** Creating custom designs on various craft materials.
- **Personalized Gifts:** Making unique and personalized gifts for special occasions.
- **Industrial and Non-Textile Uses:** Printing on non-fabric materials like wood and metal for industrial applications.

Safety and Compliance

Safety and environmental considerations are crucial when operating a DTF printer to ensure safe practices and compliance with regulations.

Safety Precautions:

- **Handling Inks and Powders:** Use appropriate personal protective equipment (PPE) such as gloves and masks when handling inks and adhesive powders.
- **Ventilation:** Ensure proper ventilation in the printing and curing areas to avoid inhalation of fumes.
- **Equipment Safety:** Follow the manufacturer's guidelines for operating and maintaining the printer and curing equipment safely.

Regulatory Compliance:

- **Ink and Material Safety:** Use inks and materials that comply with local safety and environmental regulations.
- **Waste Disposal:** Dispose of waste materials, including used films and ink cartridges, in accordance with environmental regulations.
- **Certifications:** Ensure that the printer and consumables have relevant safety certifications, such as CE or RoHS, for safe usage.

By understanding the principles, benefits, and applications of DTF printing, users can fully leverage the capabilities of their DTF printer to produce high-quality, customized prints across various mediums.2. Getting Started

Unpacking and Setup

Unpack instructions.

Unpacking a DTF (Direct-to-Film) printer requires careful handling to avoid damaging the equipment. Here's a step-by-step guide for safely unpacking and setting up your DTF printer:

Before You Start

1. **Prepare the Space**: Ensure you have a clean, flat, and spacious area to work in. This area should be free of dust and other contaminants that could affect the printer's operation.

2. **Gather Tools**: You might need a utility knife or scissors for cutting packing tape, and possibly a screwdriver if any parts are fastened.

Steps

1. **Inspect the Packaging**:

   - Check the exterior of the box for any signs of damage during shipping. Document any damage with photos before opening.

2. **Open the Box Carefully**:

   - Use a utility knife or scissors to cut through the tape sealing the box. Avoid cutting too deep to prevent damaging the contents.

3. **Remove the Accessories and Documentation**:

   - Look for any small boxes or packages containing accessories, manuals, or installation CDs. These are usually located at the top or sides of the main package. Set these aside in a safe place.

4. **Lift Out the Printer**:

   - If the printer is heavy or large, you may need assistance to lift it out safely. Some DTF printers come with handles or designated areas for lifting.
   - Hold the printer firmly by these designated lifting points to avoid any strain on delicate parts.

5. **Remove Protective Materials**:

- Carefully peel away any foam, plastic, or protective coverings surrounding the printer. Check inside and around the printer for any additional packing materials.
- Look out for packing materials securing the print head and other moving parts. These must be removed before operation.

6. **Inspect the Printer**:

- Once the printer is free from its packaging, visually inspect it for any signs of damage. Ensure all components are intact and secure.

Setting Up the Printer

1. **Position the Printer**:

- Place the printer on a stable, flat surface. Ensure it is close to power outlets and within reach of your computer or network if connecting via cables.

2. **Install Ink Cartridges and DTF Film Roll**:

- Follow the manufacturer's instructions for installing the ink cartridges and loading the DTF film. This usually involves inserting the cartridges into the designated slots and loading the film roll in the feeder.
- Remove any protective tapes or plugs from the cartridges.

3. **Connect to Power and Computer**:

- Plug in the power cord and connect the printer to your computer using the provided USB cable or via a network connection if applicable.
- Do not turn on the printer yet.

4. **Install Software and Drivers**:

- Install any necessary drivers and software from the provided CD or download them from the manufacturer's website.
- Follow the on-screen instructions to complete the installation.

5. **Power On the Printer**:

- Once the software is installed, turn on the printer. Allow it to complete its initialization process.

6. **Perform Initial Setup and Calibration**:

   - Follow the instructions in the manual for initial setup, which may include calibration and test printing.
   - Load the DTF film and run a test print to ensure everything is functioning correctly.

7. **Final Adjustments**:

   - Make any necessary adjustments to the print settings based on the test print results. This could include aligning the print head, adjusting the print resolution, or configuring the film feed.

Tips

- Save the original packaging materials in case you need to transport or return the printer.

- Always refer to the manufacturer's manual for specific instructions related to your DTF printer model.

- DTF printers contain delicate parts; handle them with care to avoid damage.

- **Issues During Setup**: Refer to the troubleshooting section of the printer's manual or contact the manufacturer's support if you encounter any issues during setup.

Check package contents.

When unpacking a DTF printer, it's crucial to verify that all components and accessories are included in the package. Here's a detailed guide on how to check the package contents:

1. **Review the Packing List or Manual**:

   - Locate the packing list or the section in the user manual that outlines all the components and accessories included with the printer. This document often accompanies the printer or is included inside the box.

2. **Organize a Clean Space**:

   - Set up a clean, flat area to lay out all the items as you unpack them. This helps in keeping track and ensuring nothing is misplaced or overlooked.

3. **Unpack and Identify Components**:

   - Carefully remove each item from the packaging and compare it against the packing list. Below is a common list of components you might find with a DTF printer:

Common Components in a DTF Printer Package

Main Components

1. **DTF Printer Unit**:

   - The main body of the printer is often protected with foam or plastic covers.
   - Check for any damage and ensure that all protective tapes and transport locks are removed before use.

2. **Ink Cartridges or Bottles**:

- Usually, DTF printers come with a set of ink cartridges or bottles (Cyan, Magenta, Yellow, Black, and White).
- Inspect for any leaks or damages.

3. **DTF Film Roll or Sheets**:

- A roll or a pack of DTF film (transparent sheets used for printing).
- Verify that the film is in good condition, without any creases or defects.

Accessories and Tools

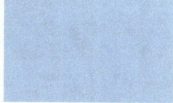

4. **Cleaning Kit**: Includes cleaning solution, wipes, and sometimes a syringe for maintaining the printer and cleaning the print head.

5. **Spare Parts**:

- This may include spare print heads, nozzles, or other small parts.

- Ensure that all spare parts are accounted for and in good condition.

6. **Power Cord**:

   - A standard power cord suitable for your region's voltage and plug type.
   - Verify that the plug matches your local electrical outlets.

7. **USB or Network Cable**:

   - Used to connect the printer to your computer or network.
   - Check that the cable is intact and fits the corresponding ports on your printer and computer.

8. **Software CD or USB Drive**:

   - Includes drivers and software needed to operate the printer.
   - If no physical media is included, instructions should guide you to download the necessary software from the manufacturer's website.

Documentation

9. **User Manual and Quick Start Guide**:

   - Printed manuals or guides that provide instructions for setting up and operating the printer.
   - Look for any additional documentation like warranty information and safety instructions.

10. **Warranty Card**:

    o A card or booklet that details the warranty terms and how to register your product for warranty coverage.

Verification

- **Cross-Check Each Item**: Match each unpacked item with the packing list. Tick off items as you verify their presence and condition.
- **Inspect for Damage**: Examine each component for signs of damage, such as cracks, dents, or leaks, especially for sensitive items like ink cartridges and the printer body.

- **Ensure Proper Quantity**: Confirm that you have the correct quantity of each item as per the packing list (e.g., the right number of ink cartridges, sheets of film, etc.).
- **Test Fitting and Functionality**: For cables and connectors, briefly test fit them into the printer and computer to ensure they fit properly.
- Do not power on or operate the printer yet, just check the physical connection.

Troubleshooting Missing or Damaged Items

- **Document Any Issues**: Take photos of any missing or damaged items for your records.

- **Contact the Seller or Manufacturer**: Report any discrepancies to the seller or manufacturer's support team immediately. Provide them with the photos and details of what is missing or damaged.

- **Keep All Packaging Materials**: Until the issue is resolved, keep all packaging materials and documentation in case they are needed for returns or further verification.

Set up the printer location and environment.

Setting up the correct location and environment for your DTF printer is crucial for its optimal performance and longevity. Here's a detailed guide to help you prepare the perfect setup:

Choose the Right Location

1. **Stable Surface**:

   o Place the printer on a sturdy, level surface that can support its weight and size. This minimizes vibrations and ensures consistent print quality.

   o Avoid placing it on uneven or shaky tables that might cause movement during operation.

2. **Adequate Space**:

- Ensure there is sufficient space around the printer for ventilation and access. DTF printers require room for both the film feed and output trays.

- Leave enough clearance for opening covers, replacing ink cartridges, and routine maintenance.

3. **Proximity to Power and Connectivity**:

- Position the printer near power outlets and, if applicable, within reach of your computer or network ports for USB or Ethernet connections.

- Avoid using extension cords or power strips that can't handle the printer's power requirements.

4. **Controlled Environment**:

- Place the printer in a clean, dust-free environment to prevent dust particles from affecting print quality.

- Avoid areas with direct sunlight, as it can heat up the printer and the ink, affecting performance.

Environmental Conditions

1. **Temperature and Humidity**:

- Maintain a stable room temperature between 15°C to 30°C (59°F to 86°F) and humidity levels between 40% and 60%.

- Extreme temperatures and humidity can cause the ink to behave unpredictably, affect film adhesion, and damage electronic components.

2. **Ventilation**:

- Ensure proper ventilation to disperse any fumes from inks and adhesives used in the printing process.

- Consider using air purifiers or exhaust fans if the area is enclosed.

3. **Avoid Interference**:

- o Keep the printer away from other electronic devices that may emit electromagnetic interference, such as microwaves or large motors.

- o Do not place it near devices that generate heat, like radiators or stoves.

Preparing the Workspace

1. **Clean the Area**:

   - o Clean the surface where the printer will be placed, and ensure the surrounding area is free from dust and debris.

   - o Regularly maintain the cleanliness of the workspace to prevent contaminants from affecting the printer.

2. **Organize Accessories**:

   - o Arrange all necessary accessories, such as ink cartridges, film rolls, and cleaning supplies, within easy reach but in an organized manner.

   - o Use shelves or storage bins to keep items organized and off the main work surface.

3. **Secure Cables and Connections**:

   - o Route power and data cables neatly to avoid tripping hazards and to keep them from tangling.

   - o Use cable ties or clips to manage excess cable length.

4. **Prepare for Waste Disposal**:

   - o Set up a waste disposal area for discarded film sheets and used ink cartridges.

   - o Have a plan for environmentally friendly disposal or recycling of these materials.

Set Up the Printer

- • Carefully position the printer on the chosen surface. Make sure it is stable and doesn't wobble.

- Double-check that all transport locks and protective materials have been removed.
- Plug the printer into a dedicated outlet. Avoid using outlets that are heavily loaded with other devices.
- Ensure the power cord is securely connected and free from damage.

1. **Install Ink and Film**:

   - Follow the manufacturer's instructions to install the ink cartridges and load the DTF film.
   - Handle ink cartridges and film with clean, dry hands to avoid contamination.

2. **Connect to Computer or Network**:

   - Use the provided USB cable or connect via Ethernet if your printer supports network connectivity.
   - Make sure the connections are secure and the cables are not strained or bent sharply.

3. **Software and Driver Installation**:

   - Install the necessary drivers and software from the provided CD or download them from the manufacturer's website.
   - Follow the setup wizard to configure the printer on your computer.

4. **Calibrate and Test**:

   - Power on the printer and allow it to go through its initial setup process.
   - Perform any required calibration procedures, such as aligning the print head or adjusting print settings.
   - Run a test print to ensure everything is functioning correctly.

Maintain the Environment

- Dust and clean the printer and its surrounding area regularly to maintain a dust-free environment.
- Clean the print heads and other critical parts as recommended by the manufacturer.

- Use a thermometer and hygrometer to keep track of temperature and humidity.
- Adjust the room's climate control as necessary to maintain optimal conditions.
- Ensure the printer is in a secure location to prevent unauthorized access or tampering.
- Keep liquids and other potential hazards away from the printer.

Hardware Installation

Assembly instructions (if required).

Depending on the model, your DTF printer may require some assembly before it's ready for use. Below are the general steps and tips to help you assemble your DTF printer. Always refer to the specific instructions provided in your printer's user manual for detailed guidance.

Tools You Might Need:

- Screwdrivers (Phillips and flathead)

- Allen wrench set

- Utility knife or scissors

- Cleaning cloth

Assembling the Printer Base and Frame

1. **Set Up the Base**:

   o If your printer comes with a base or stand, assemble it first. This usually involves attaching legs or supports to the main base.

   o Use the screws and tools provided, following the instructions to secure each part firmly.

2. **Attach the Printer Frame**:

- o Position the main printer body on the assembled base or directly on your work surface if it doesn't have a separate base.

- o Secure the printer frame to the base using the screws or bolts provided. Ensure the frame is stable and level.

3. **Install Support Brackets** (if applicable):

- o Attach any support brackets or stabilizers included with the printer. These are often used to reinforce the frame or secure large components like the print head assembly.

Installing the Print Head Assembly

1. **Position the Print Head**:

- • Carefully remove the print head assembly from its packaging. Avoid touching the print nozzles to prevent damage.
- • Align the print head with its mounting bracket or carriage on the printer.

2. **Secure the Print Head**:

- o Use the screws or clips provided to attach the print head assembly to the carriage. Tighten securely but do not over-tighten as this could damage the print head.

3. **Connect the Cables**:

o Attach the print head's data and power cables to their respective ports on the printer. These connections are usually colour-coded or labelled for easy identification.

o Ensure all connections are secure and there are no loose wires.

Assembling the Ink System

- If the ink system includes external tanks, place them in their designated holders or compartments.
- Connect the ink lines from the tanks to the print head assembly as specified in the manual. Secure the connections to prevent leaks.
- Insert each ink cartridge into its respective slot on the printer. Follow the color-coded labels to match each cartridge correctly.
- Push each cartridge until it clicks into place.
- Use the printer's control panel or software to prime the ink system. This process fills the ink lines and prepares the print head for use.
- Check for any air bubbles or leaks in the ink lines.

Set Up the DTF Film Holder

- Attach any required brackets or supports to hold the DTF film roll. This might include mounting spindles, rollers, or tension bars.
- Ensure the film holder is aligned properly with the printer's film feed mechanism.

- Place the film roll onto the holder and guide the leading edge of the film into the feed mechanism.
- Adjust the tension and alignment to ensure the film feeds smoothly and evenly into the printer.

6. Connecting the Dryer or Curing Unit (if applicable)

- **Position the Dryer/Curing Unit**: Place the dryer or curing unit near the printer where the printed film will exit. Ensure it's on a stable surface and aligned with the printer's output path.
- **Connect Power and Control Cables**: Attach the power cord to the dryer or curing unit and plug it into a suitable outlet.
- If the unit connects to the printer for synchronized operation, connect any control cables as per the manufacturer's instructions.
- **Test the Dryer/Curing Function**: Turn on the dryer or curing unit and check its functionality. Adjust temperature and timing settings as required for your printing process.

Final Checks

- Attach any remaining covers or panels to the printer. These often include side panels, top covers, or protective shields for moving parts.
- Secure each panel with the screws or fasteners provided.
- Verify that all screws, bolts, and connections are secure. Check for any loose parts or missing components.
- Connect the printer to a power source and turn it on. Allow the printer to initialize and complete any self-checks.
- Run a test print or perform initial calibration to ensure everything is functioning correctly.
- Install any necessary software and drivers on your computer. Connect the printer via USB or network as per the instructions.
- Configure the printer settings in the software to match your specific needs.

Connecting cables and power supply.

Connecting the cables and power supply to your DTF printer is a crucial step in the installation process. Proper connections ensure that your printer communicates correctly with your computer and operates safely. Below is a detailed guide to help you connect your DTF printer's cables and power supply.

Steps for Connecting Cables and Power Supply

1. **Ensure Safety**:
   - o Make sure your printer is placed on a stable, level surface.
   - o Ensure that the printer is turned off and unplugged from the power source before connecting any cables.

2. **Prepare the Cables**:
   - o Gather all necessary cables: power cord, USB or Ethernet cable (for data connection), and any additional cables for accessories like the curing unit or external ink system.
   - o Inspect the cables for any visible damage and ensure they are appropriate for your printer and computer.

Connecting the Power Supply

1. **Locate the Power Input**:
   - o Find the power input port on the printer. This is typically at the back or side of the printer.
   - o Check the voltage requirement specified on the printer to ensure compatibility with your local power supply.

2. **Connect the Power Cord**:
   - o Plug one end of the power cord into the printer's power input port.
   - o Plug the other end into a wall outlet or a surge protector that meets the power requirements of your printer.

3. **Secure the Connection**:
   - o Ensure the power cord is securely connected at both ends.
   - o Avoid placing the cord under any stress or bending it sharply.

3. Data Connection to Computer

1. **USB Connection** (Common for most printers):

   o   Locate the USB port on the printer. This is usually at the back or side.

   o   Connect one end of the USB cable to the printer's USB port.

   o   Connect the other end to an available USB port on your computer.

   o   Ensure the USB cable is firmly connected and not loose.

2. **Ethernet Connection** (If your printer supports network connectivity):

   o   Locate the Ethernet port on the printer.

   o   Connect one end of the Ethernet cable to the printer's Ethernet port.

   o   Connect the other end to a network switch, router, or directly to your computer's Ethernet port.

   o   Verify that the Ethernet cable clicks into place and is securely connected.

3. **Wireless Connection** (If applicable):

   o   For printers with wireless capabilities, you may need to configure the wireless settings through the printer's control panel or software.

   o   Follow the manufacturer's instructions to connect the printer to your Wi-Fi network.

   o   Ensure that your computer is on the same network for proper communication.

Connect Additional Components

1. **Curing Unit or Dryer**:

   • If your setup includes a curing unit or dryer, connect its power cord to a suitable power outlet.
   • Connect any control or synchronization cables between the printer and the curing unit as specified in the manual.

2. **External Ink System**:

- If using an external ink system, connect the ink tubes securely to their designated ports on the printer.
- Follow the manufacturer's instructions for any electrical connections required for the ink system's operation.

5. Managing and Securing Cables

- Organize the cables to prevent tangling and ensure they don't interfere with printer operation.
- Use cable ties or clips to bundle excess cable length neatly.
- Ensure that cables are not crossing over or near high-power electrical equipment that could cause interference.
- Keep the data cables separate from the power cables to minimize potential electromagnetic interference.
- Place cables out of walkways and secure them to avoid tripping hazards.
- Use cable organizers or conduits to keep the workspace tidy and safe.

Troubleshooting Common Issues

1. **No Power**:

- Ensure the power cord is securely connected to both the printer and the power source.
- Check that the power outlet is functioning by testing it with another device.
- Verify that any power switches on the printer or surge protector are turned on.

2. **No Data Connection**:

- Re-check the USB or Ethernet cable connections. Ensure they are securely plugged in.
- For USB connections, try using a different USB port on your computer.
- For network connections, verify that the printer and computer are on the same network and check the network settings.

3. **Interference or Poor Performance**:

- Ensure that cables are not placed near sources of electromagnetic interference.
- Check for updates to the printer's firmware and drivers, which can resolve connectivity and performance issues.

Software Installation

Downloading and Installing Printer Drivers for Your DTF Printer

Printer drivers are essential software that allows your computer to communicate with your Direct-to-Film printer. Properly installing these drivers ensures your printer functions correctly and takes full advantage of its features. Follow these detailed steps to download and install the printer drivers for your DTF printer.

1. **Check System Requirements**:

   - Ensure your computer meets the system requirements for the printer drivers. These are usually listed on the printer's box or the manufacturer's website.
   - Confirm compatibility with your operating system (Windows, macOS, Linux).

2. **Gather Necessary Information**:

   - Identify your printer model and serial number. This information is usually found on a label on the printer or in the user manual.
   - Have your computer's operating system version handy, as this will determine the correct driver to download.

3. **Establish an Internet Connection**:

   - Make sure your computer is connected to the internet to download the drivers from the manufacturer's website.

2. Downloading the Printer Drivers

1. **Visit the Manufacturer's Website**:

   - Go to the official website of your DTF printer's manufacturer. Use a search engine if you're unsure of the URL.
   - Navigate to the "Support" or "Downloads" section of the website.

2. **Find Your Printer Model**:

   - Use the search function or browse through the list of products to find your specific printer model.
   - Select your printer model to access its support page, where you can find driver downloads and other resources.

3. **Select the Correct Driver**:

   - Choose the driver that matches your computer's operating system and version. Manufacturers often provide drivers for different OS versions, so make sure you select the right one.
   - Click the download link to save the driver installation file to your computer.

4. **Download Additional Software** (if needed):

   - Some printers come with additional software for advanced features or maintenance tasks. Download any recommended utilities or software provided on the driver page.

3. Installing the Printer Drivers

   - Once the driver download is complete, locate the file in your computer's "Downloads" folder or the location you specified.
   - Double-click the downloaded driver file to start the installation process. This file is typically an executable (.exe) on Windows or a package (.pkg) on macOS.
   - If prompted by your operating system, confirm that you want to run the file.
   - The installation wizard will guide you through the setup process. Follow the on-screen instructions carefully.
   - Accept the license agreement, choose the installation location if prompted, and select any additional components you want to install.
   - During the installation, you may be prompted to connect your printer to the computer. Make sure the printer is turned on and connected via USB, Ethernet, or Wi-Fi as required.
   - The installer will attempt to detect the printer and complete the setup.

- Once the installation process is complete, you may be asked to restart your computer. Do so to ensure the drivers are fully integrated into your system.
- Check for any final on-screen instructions or configurations to complete the setup.

Configuring the Printer

1. **Set as Default Printer**:

   - After the installation, set your DTF printer as the default printer in your computer's settings. This ensures that print jobs are sent to the correct printer by default.
   - On Windows, go to "Settings" > "Devices" > "Printers & scanners" and select your printer as the default.
   - On macOS, go to "System Preferences" > "Printers & Scanners" and set your printer as the default.

2. **Print a Test Page**:

   - Use the printer's control panel or the computer's printer settings to print a test page. This verifies that the printer is correctly connected and the drivers are functioning properly.
   - Check the quality of the print and ensure all colours and details are accurate.

3. **Adjust Printer Settings**:

   - Open the printer's properties or preferences from your computer's printer settings to configure any additional options like print quality, paper size, or ink usage.
   - Save your preferred settings for future print jobs.

Updating and Maintaining Drivers

- Periodically visit the manufacturer's website to check for updated drivers or software. Updated drivers can improve performance, add features, or fix issues.
- Enable automatic update notifications if available.
- If you encounter issues with your printer, consider reinstalling the drivers. Uninstall the current drivers from your computer's settings and then follow the steps to download and install the latest version.

- On Windows, you can uninstall drivers via "Control Panel" > "Programs" > "Uninstall a program."
- On macOS, remove the printer from the "Printers & Scanners" preferences and then reinstall the drivers.
- **Backup and Restore**: Keep a backup of your printer drivers, especially if you rely on specific settings or configurations. This is useful for quick reinstallation if you encounter problems.

6. Troubleshooting Common Driver Installation Issues

1. **Driver Not Found**:

   - Ensure you've downloaded the correct driver for your printer model and operating system version.
   - Check the manufacturer's support page for any special instructions or updates.

2. **Printer Not Detected**:

   - Verify that the printer is turned on and properly connected to your computer.
   - Try a different USB port or check your network connections if using Ethernet or Wi-Fi.

3. **Installation Errors**:

   - Close any other applications that might interfere with the installation process.
   - Run the installer as an administrator if on Windows. Right-click the installation file and select "Run as administrator."

4. **Compatibility Issues**:

   - Ensure your operating system is up to date. Sometimes, outdated OS versions can cause compatibility issues with new drivers.
   - Check if there are any beta or alternative drivers available for your OS version.

Installing DTF-specific software (RIP software, design tools).

When installing software for direct-to-film (DTF) printing, typically involves several steps and components to ensure the system is properly set up for optimal operation. Here's a guide to help you through the process:

1. **RIP Software (Raster Image Processor):**

   - Converts design files into formats that DTF printers can interpret.
   - Manages colour profiles, ink settings, and print layouts.
   - Examples: **Acrorip, Cadlink Digital Factory**, or **Epson Edge Print**.

2. **Design Software:**

   - Used to create and edit designs before they are processed by RIP software.
   - Examples: **Adobe Photoshop, Illustrator, CorelDRAW**, or free alternatives like **GIMP** and **Inkscape**.

1. Install Design Software:

   - Visit the official website of the design software of your choice (e.g., Adobe for Photoshop).
   - Follow the provided installation steps.

- **Configure Settings:**

   - Set up your workspace and preferences.
   - Familiarize yourself with the tools and features needed for DTF design, such as managing layers, colour modes, and file formats (e.g., PNG, TIFF).

2. Install RIP Software:

   - **Purchase/Download:** Acquire the RIP software from the official source or authorized distributors.
   - Run the installer file and follow the on-screen instructions.
   - Enter any necessary license keys or activation codes.

- **Configuration:**

   - Connect your DTF printer to the computer.
   - Configure printer settings within the RIP software.
   - Set up colour profiles specific to your printer and DTF inks.
   - Customize ink limits, and resolution settings, and adjust print head settings.

- **Test and Calibrate:**
  - Perform initial test prints to calibrate colour and ink usage.
  - Adjust settings as needed to match the desired print quality.

Additional Tips:

- Ensure your computer meets the minimum requirements for both the design and RIP software.
- Adequate RAM, processing power, and storage space are critical for smooth operation.
- Utilize tutorials, user manuals, and customer support offered by software providers.
- Online communities and forums can also be valuable resources for troubleshooting and tips.
- Regularly back up your settings and designs.
- Keep both software and firmware up to date to benefit from new features and fixes.

Resources for Popular RIP Software:

- **Acrorip**: Acrorip Installation Guide

- **Cadlink Digital Factory**: Cadlink Software Setup

- **Epson Edge Print**: Epson Edge Print Setup

Following these steps should help you get your DTF printing system set up and running efficiently.

Initial Calibration

Loading film and ink cartridges.

Loading film and ink cartridges into a DTF printer involves precise steps to ensure smooth operation and high-quality prints. Here's a detailed guide for both processes:

1. **Prepare the Film:**
   - Ensure the film is compatible with your DTF printer.
   - Handle the film by the edges to avoid fingerprints and dust.

2. **Unwind and Load the Film Roll:**

- Place the roll on the designated holder or spindle.
- Make sure the film unwinds in the correct direction. The printable side usually faces up.
- Align the film with the printer's feed guides.
- Pull the film forward until it reaches the feed rollers or sensors.
- Adjust the side guides to ensure the film feeds straight.
- Lock the guides in place to prevent shifting during printing.

3. **Feed the Film into the Printer:**

- **Automatic Feed (if available):** Use the printer's film load button or interface to automatically pull the film through the rollers.
- **Manual Feed:** Gently push the film until it engages with the feed rollers.
- Continue feeding until the film is properly positioned inside the printer.
- **Check the Film Tension:** Ensure the film is neither too loose nor too tight. Adjust tension settings if necessary.
- **Test the Feed:** Run a small piece of film through the printer to check for smooth feeding.
- Adjust the guides and tension if the film does not feed properly.

Loading Ink Cartridges into a DTF Printer

1. **Prepare the Ink Cartridges:**

- Use cartridges specifically designed for your DTF printer model.
- Gently shake the cartridges if required (as per the manufacturer's instructions) to mix the ink evenly.

2. **Access the Cartridge Slots:**

- Open the printer's ink cartridge compartment.
- This is usually located at the front or side of the printer. Refer to your printer's manual for the exact location.

3. **Remove Old Cartridges (if replacing):**

- Push the release lever or button to eject the old cartridges.
- Carefully remove them to avoid ink spills.

4. **Insert New Cartridges:**

- Align each cartridge with its corresponding slot.
- Push the cartridge in until it clicks into place.
- Ensure each cartridge is firmly seated and the labels or colours match the slots.

5. **Close the Compartment:**

- Close the ink cartridge compartment securely.

6. **Prime the Ink System (if necessary):**

- Some printers require priming to fill the ink lines and nozzles with the new ink.
- Follow the printer's instructions for priming the ink system.

7. **Run a Test Print:**

- Print a test page to check the ink flow and print quality.
- Perform any required nozzle checks or cleaning cycles if the print quality is not optimal.

Additional Tips:

- Use gloves when handling ink cartridges and film to prevent ink stains and contamination.
- Ensure your printer firmware is up to date to support the latest ink and film compatibility.
- Always use manufacturer-recommended ink and film to maintain print quality and avoid damage to the printer.
- Store film and ink cartridges in a cool, dry place to preserve their quality and lifespan.

Troubleshooting Common Issues:

- **Film Feeding Problems:**

  - Recheck the alignment and tension of the film.
  - Clean the feed rollers to remove dust or residue.

- **Ink Flow Issues:**

  - Perform nozzle checks and cleaning cycles.
  - Ensure cartridges are not expired or clogged.

Detailed initial printer calibration.

Calibrating your Direct to Film (DTF) printer to achieve accurate colours, proper alignment, and high-quality prints, should follow the following steps:

1. **Power Up and Connect:**

   - **Turn on the Printer:** Make sure the printer is plugged in and turned on.
   - **Connect to the Computer:** Ensure the printer is properly connected to the computer via USB or network.

2. **Install and Open RIP Software:**

   - **Install the Software:** If not already installed, install your chosen RIP software (e.g., Acrorip, Cadlink Digital Factory).
   - **Launch the Software:** Open the RIP software and make sure it recognizes your printer.
   - **Load Media and Ink:** Load the Film and follow the steps outlined in the previous section to load the film into the printer.
   - **Install the Ink Cartridges:** Make sure all ink cartridges are installed correctly and contain enough ink for the calibration process.

3. **Perform Nozzle Check:**

   - **Access Nozzle Check:** Use the printer's control panel or the RIP software to start a nozzle check.
   - **Print the Nozzle Pattern:** The printer will print a pattern that shows if any nozzles are clogged.
   - **Inspect the Pattern:** Look for any missing lines or gaps.
   - **Clean Nozzles (if necessary):** If there are issues, perform a nozzle cleaning cycle using the printer's maintenance menu and repeat the nozzle check until it's clear.

4. **Print Head Alignment:**

   - **Access Print Head Alignment:** Use the printer's control panel or the RIP software to start the print head alignment process.
   - **Print Alignment Pattern:** The printer will print a series of lines or blocks.
   - **Adjust Alignment:** Follow the prompts to adjust the alignment based on the printed pattern.

- **Repeat (if needed):** Perform additional alignment steps if the initial results are not satisfactory.

5. **Colour Calibration:**

   - **Print Color Charts:** Use the RIP software to print colour calibration charts on your DTF film.
   - **Measure the Colors:** Use a spectrophotometer or colourimeter (if available) to measure the colours on the printed chart.
   - **Adjust Color Profiles:** Input the measurements into the RIP software to adjust the printer's colour profile.
   - This process ensures that the colours you print match the design on your screen as closely as possible.

6. **Ink Density Calibration:**

   - **Access Ink Settings:** In the RIP software, navigate to the ink settings or ink limits section.
   - **Print Density Test:** Print a series of tests to determine the optimal ink density for each colour.
   - **Adjust Ink Limits:** Adjust the ink limits based on the test results to avoid oversaturation and bleeding.

7. **ICC Profile Configuration:**

   - **Load ICC Profiles:** Install ICC profiles provided by the ink or media manufacturer.
   - **Apply Profiles:** Apply the appropriate ICC profile in the RIP software for accurate colour reproduction.

8. **Print a Test Image:**

   - **Select a Test File:** Choose a test image that includes a range of colours, gradients, and details.
   - **Print the Image:** Use the RIP software to send the image to the printer.
   - **Evaluate Print Quality:** Check for color accuracy, alignment, and overall quality.
   - **Make Final Adjustments:** Adjust any settings as needed to improve print quality.

Additional Tips for Effective Calibration:

- Perform regular maintenance checks, such as nozzle cleaning and alignment, to keep your printer in top condition.
- Keep your printing environment stable. Temperature and humidity can affect print quality.
- Always use good quality DTF film and ink to ensure consistent results.
- Keep a log of the settings used during calibration for future reference.
- If calibration issues persist, consult your printer's support team or a professional technician.

Detailed Test Printing And Troubleshooting Initial Setup Procedure

After completing the initial calibration of your DTF printer, it's crucial to perform a test print to ensure everything is functioning correctly. This process helps identify any issues early on and allows for troubleshooting and fine-tuning. Here's a step-by-step guide to performing a test print and addressing common problems during the initial setup:

- **Select a Test Image:** Choose a test image that includes a wide range of colours, gradients, and fine details. Many DTF printing guides provide standard test files, or you can use an image with a mix of graphic elements and text.
- **Prepare the File:** Open the test image in your design software and check that it meets the necessary specifications (e.g., resolution, size, and colour mode).
- Save the file in a compatible format (e.g., PNG, TIFF).
- **Load the Film:** Make sure the DTF film is properly loaded and aligned in the printer as per the previous instructions.
- **Check Ink Levels:** Confirm that the ink cartridges have enough ink and are properly installed.

Configure RIP Software Settings:

- Open your RIP software and load the test image.
- Set the appropriate print settings, including:

  - **Media Type**: Select the correct film type.

  - **Print Quality**: Choose the desired print resolution.

- **Color Profile**: Apply the correct ICC profile.

- **Ink Density**: Ensure the ink limits are properly set.

2. **Send the Print Job:**

- Send the test print job from the RIP software to the printer.
- Monitor the printer to ensure the film feeds smoothly and the print process begins without issues.
- **Inspect the Test Print:** Once printed, carefully examine the output for:

  - **Colour Accuracy**: Colors should match the original design.

  - **Print Quality**: Look for sharpness and clarity in details.

  - **Uniformity**: Check for an even distribution of ink without streaks or blotches.

  - **Alignment**: Ensure there are no misalignments or banding.

Troubleshooting Common Issues:

1. **Colour Inaccuracy:**
Problem: Colors don't match the original design.

Solution:

- Verify that the correct ICC profile is applied.
- Recheck colour settings in the RIP software.
- Ensure the film and inks are compatible and not expired.

2. **Banding or Lines:**
Problem: Horizontal or vertical lines appear in the print.

Solution:

- Perform a print head cleaning or alignment procedure.
- Check for any obstructions or debris in the print path.
- Ensure the film is loaded correctly without tension issues.

3. **Ink Smudging or Bleeding:**
Problem: Ink appears smudged or spreads beyond the intended areas.

Solution:

- Reduce ink density settings in the RIP software.
- Allow more drying time between print passes.
- Check if the film is compatible with your ink and set up correctly.

4. **Poor Print Quality:**

Problem: The print appears blurry or pixelated.

Solution:

- Increase the print resolution setting in the RIP software.
- Ensure the original image file is high-resolution and properly prepared.
- Verify that the printer's print heads are clean and functioning correctly.

5. **Misalignment:**

Problem: Prints are skewed or not aligned properly.

Solution:

- Recheck the alignment settings and guides in the printer.
- Confirm the film is feeding straight and is not skewed.
- Re-run the print head alignment process.

6. **Film Feeding Issues:**

Problem: The film is not feeding smoothly or jams.

Solution:

- Re-align the film and adjust tension if necessary.
- Clean the feed rollers and ensure they are free from dust or residue.
- Verify that the film is compatible with your printer's feed system.

Regular Maintenance and Follow-Up:

- Perform regular nozzle checks and cleanings to prevent clogging and maintain print quality.
- Periodically recalibrate the printer to adjust for any changes in the environment or media.
- Keep your RIP software and printer firmware updated to benefit from improvements and fixes.

- Keep a log of any issues and solutions for future reference and to help with troubleshooting.

Operating the Printer

Printer Controls and Interface

Common Components of a DTF Printer Control Panel

Understanding the printer control panel and display is essential for managing your DTF printer effectively. This overview will cover the common elements found on DTF printer control panels and how to use them for routine operations, maintenance, and troubleshooting.

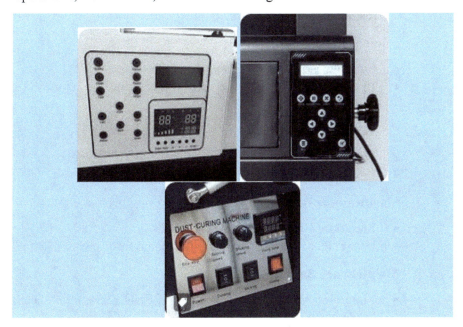

1. **Power Button:**

    - **Function**: Turns the printer on and off.
    - **Usage**: Press to start up or shut down the printer. Ensure proper shutdown to avoid damaging the printer.

2. **Menu Button:**

    - **Function**: Accesses the main menu for various settings and functions.
    - **Usage**: Navigate through different printer options such as settings, maintenance, and network configurations.

3. **Navigation Buttons:**

- **Function**: Allows scrolling through menus and options.
- **Usage**: Typically includes directional arrows (up, down, left, right) and an OK or Enter button to select items.

4. **Display Screen:**

- **Function**: Shows the current status, menu options, and error messages.
- **Usage**: View and select settings, monitor printing progress, and read notifications.

5. **Home Button:**

- **Function**: Returns to the main or home screen.
- **Usage**: Press to quickly exit the current menu and return to the default screen.

6. **Cancel/Stop Button:**

- **Function**: Stops ongoing print jobs or cancels operations.
- **Usage**: Use to halt printing immediately if needed.

7. **Start/Resume Button:**

- **Function**: Begins or resumes print jobs.
- **Usage**: Press to start a print job or resume from a paused state.

8. **Maintenance Button:**

- **Function**: Accesses maintenance functions like nozzle checks, head cleaning, and alignment.
- **Usage**: Perform regular maintenance tasks to keep the printer in good working condition.

9. **Ink Levels Button:**

- **Function**: Checks the current ink levels.
- **Usage**: View the status of ink cartridges to ensure there is enough ink for upcoming print jobs.

10. **Film Feed Button:**

- **Function**: Manages the loading and feeding of film.

- **Usage**: Advance or retract film to ensure it is properly positioned for printing.

Using the Control Panel for Common Operations

1. **Initial Setup and Configuration:**

   - **Power On**: Press the power button to start the printer.
   - **Navigate to Settings**: Use the menu and navigation buttons to access system settings.
   - **Set Language and Preferences**: Configure the display language, units, and other basic preferences.

2. **Loading and Ejecting Film:**

   - **Load Film**: Use the film feed button to manually load the film. Ensure it aligns correctly with the guides.
   - **Eject Film**: If needed, use the reverse function or manually feed the film out of the printer.

3. **Starting and Managing Print Jobs:**

   - **Start Print Job**: Send the print job from the RIP software. Use the start/resume button if needed.
   - **Pause/Resume**: Use the pause button to temporarily halt printing, then press resume to continue.
   - **Cancel Print Job**: Press the cancel button to stop a print job in progress.

4. **Performing Maintenance:**

   - **Access Maintenance Menu**: Navigate to the maintenance section using the menu button.
   - **Run Nozzle Check**: Select the nozzle check option to print a pattern and check for any clogs.
   - **Clean Print Heads**: Use the head cleaning function if the nozzle check indicates issues.
   - **Align Print Heads**: Perform print head alignment to ensure proper print quality.

5. **Checking Ink and Film Status:**

- **View Ink Levels**: Press the ink levels button to check the status of each cartridge.
- **Monitor Film Usage**: Use the display to keep track of film usage and adjust as needed.

6. **Handling Errors and Alerts:**

- **Read Error Messages**: Use the display to understand any error codes or messages.
- **Follow On-Screen Instructions**: Many printers provide step-by-step guidance to resolve issues.

Advanced Features (Specific to Some Models)

1. **Network and Wireless Settings:**

- **Wi-Fi Setup**: Access network settings to connect the printer to a Wi-Fi network.
- **Ethernet Configuration**: Set up wired network connections through the control panel.

2. **Firmware Updates:**

- **Check for Updates**: Use the control panel to check and install firmware updates.
- **USB Updates**: Some printers allow firmware updates via USB; follow the on-screen instructions.

3. **Custom Print Settings:**

- **Profile Management**: Load and manage custom print profiles for different media and ink setups.
- **Advanced Calibration**: Access detailed calibration settings for precise adjustments.

Tips for Efficient Use:

- **Regularly Check the Display**: Keep an eye on the display for any alerts or messages that may require action.

- **Familiarize with the Manual**: Refer to the printer's manual for detailed explanations of each function.

- **Perform Routine Maintenance**: Use the control panel's maintenance options to keep the printer in optimal condition.

- **Update Software and Firmware**: Regularly check for updates to ensure you have the latest features and fixes.

Basic navigation and menu functions.

Navigating the menu functions of DTF printers is essential for efficient operation and maintenance. While the exact layout and options can vary between different models and brands, most DTF printers share common menu functions. Here's a basic guide to help you understand and navigate the typical menu functions found on DTF printers:

Overview of Basic Navigation:

1. **Powering On and Off:**

   - **Power Button**: Located on the control panel, press to turn the printer on or off.
   - **Proper Shutdown**: Always use the power button for shutdown to avoid damaging the printer.

2. **Accessing the Main Menu:**

   - **Menu Button**: Press to enter the main menu. This button might be labelled as "Menu" or represented by a menu icon (≡).
   - **Navigation Buttons**: Use directional arrows or a rotary dial to scroll through menu options.

3. **Selecting Menu Options:**

   - **OK/Enter Button**: Press to select or confirm a menu option.
   - **Back/Cancel Button**: Press to go back to the previous menu or cancel an action.

Common Menu Functions:

1. **Status and Information:**

   - **Status Screen**: Displays current printer status, such as "Ready," "Printing," or "Error."
   - **Ink Levels**: Shows the remaining ink for each cartridge.

- **Film Status**: Indicates the current position and length of the loaded film.

2. **Print Setup:**

   - **Print Quality**: Choose between different print resolutions and quality settings (e.g., Draft, Standard, High Quality).
   - **Media Type**: Select the type of DTF film being used, which adjusts settings for optimal printing.
   - **Print Mode**: Set up print modes such as single-pass or multi-pass printing, depending on the job requirements.

3. **Maintenance:**

   - **Nozzle Check**: Print a test pattern to check for clogged or misfiring nozzles.
   - **Head Cleaning**: Clean the print head to resolve any nozzle issues detected in the nozzle check.
   - **Print Head Alignment**: Align the print heads to ensure accurate and high-quality prints.
   - **Ink Purge**: Perform an ink purge to remove air bubbles and ensure consistent ink flow.

4. **Calibration:**

   - **Colour Calibration**: Adjust the printer's colour output to match the expected colours in your prints.
   - **Density Calibration**: Set the ink density to avoid oversaturation or under-inking on the film.

5. **Film Handling:**

   - **Load/Unload Film**: Navigate options to load or eject the DTF film from the printer.
   - **Advance/Retract Film**: Manually feed the film forward or backwards to align it properly.

6. **Network and Connectivity:**

   - **Wi-Fi Setup**: Connect the printer to a wireless network for remote printing and management.
   - **Ethernet Configuration**: Set up and manage wired network connections.

- **USB Connection**: Manage settings for direct USB connections to a computer or storage device.

7. **System Settings:**

   - **Language**: Choose the display language for the control panel.
   - **Date and Time**: Set the printer's internal clock for accurate timestamping of print jobs.
   - **Units of Measure**: Select the preferred units for measurements (e.g., inches or millimetres).

8. **Error Handling:**

   - **View Error Logs**: Check the log for recent errors or issues that have occurred.
   - **Guided Troubleshooting**: Follow on-screen instructions to resolve common problems like paper jams or ink issues.

9. **Advanced Settings:**

   - **Firmware Update**: Check for and install firmware updates to keep the printer's software current.
   - **Custom Profiles**: Load and manage custom print profiles tailored to specific media and ink types.
   - **Security Settings**: Set up user permissions and security features to control access to the printer.

Navigating Through Menus:

1. **Entering a Menu:**

   - Press the **Menu Button** to open the main menu.
   - Use the **Navigation Buttons** to scroll through the list of available options.

2. **Selecting and Adjusting Settings:**

   - Highlight the desired option using the **Up/Down Arrows**.
   - Press **OK/Enter** to select the option.
   - Use the **Left/Right Arrows** to adjust the setting or move through the submenus.

3. **Saving and Exiting:**

- Once you've made changes, press **OK/Enter** to save.
- Use the **Back/Cancel Button** to exit and return to the previous menu or the main screen.

Understanding and efficiently navigating the control panel menus of your DTF printer will help you optimize its performance and manage it more effectively.

Preparing Design Files

Supported file formats and software recommendations.

Direct-to-film printing is a versatile and relatively new method in the printing industry, allowing for high-quality prints on various fabrics. For efficiency, the right file formats and software are to be used. Here's a detailed overview of the supported file formats and software recommendations.

DTF printers typically support the following file formats:

1. **PNG (Portable Network Graphics)**

   - **Pros**: Supports transparency, lossless compression, and maintains high quality.
   - **Usage**: Ideal for designs with transparent backgrounds and high detail.

2. **JPEG/JPG (Joint Photographic Experts Group)**

   - **Pros**: Widely supported, good for detailed images.
   - **Cons**: Lossy compression, does not support transparency.
   - **Usage**: Suitable for images where file size is a concern and transparency isn't needed.

3. **TIFF (Tagged Image File Format)**

   - **Pros**: High-quality, supports multiple layers, lossless compression.
   - **Usage**: Used for high-resolution prints where maintaining quality is paramount.

4. **PDF (Portable Document Format)**

   - **Pros**: Supports vector and raster graphics, and preserves design integrity.

- **Usage**: Often used for complex designs with multiple elements.

5. **PSD (Photoshop Document)**

   - **Pros**: Supports layers, high resolution, integrates well with Adobe software.
   - **Usage**: Ideal for detailed and multi-layered designs created in Adobe Photoshop.

6. **EPS (Encapsulated PostScript)**

   - **Pros**: Supports vector graphics, scalable without quality loss.
   - **Usage**: Best for logos and designs that require scaling.

7. **AI (Adobe Illustrator)**

   - **Pros**: Vector-based, supports scaling without losing quality.
   - **Usage**: Suitable for creating and editing vector graphics, preferred for illustrations and logos.

Software Recommendations

1. **Adobe Photoshop**

   - **Usage**: Primarily for raster graphics, image editing, and design creation.
   - **Pros**: Robust editing tools, wide file format support, extensive resources and plugins.

2. **Adobe Illustrator**

   - **Usage**: Vector graphic design, creating logos, illustrations, and scalable designs.
   - **Pros**: Excellent for vector graphics, integrates well with other Adobe products.

3. **CorelDRAW**

   - **Usage**: Vector graphic design, page layout, and versatile for various types of design work.
   - **Pros**: Intuitive interface, powerful vector tools, supports a wide range of file formats.

4. **Affinity Designer**

   - **Usage**: Vector and raster graphic design.

- **Pros**: Cost-effective alternative to Adobe products, supports both vector and raster graphics, high performance.

5. **Procreate**

   - **Usage**: Digital illustration and painting (mainly for iPad users).
   - **Pros**: Intuitive interface for drawing, supports high-resolution output, affordable.

6. **Silhouette Studio**

   - **Usage**: Design software primarily used with cutting machines, useful for creating DTF transfer designs.
   - **Pros**: User-friendly, good for designing cut patterns, works well with DTF printing.

7. **GIMP (GNU Image Manipulation Program)**

   - **Usage**: Open-source image editor.
   - **Pros**: Free, supports a wide range of file formats, good alternative to Adobe Photoshop.

8. **Inkscape**

   - **Usage**: Open-source vector graphic editor.
   - **Pros**: Free, powerful vector tools, suitable for creating scalable graphics.

9. **RIP Software (Raster Image Processor)**

   - **Examples**: AcroRip, EK Print Studio, and Kothari PrintPro.
   - **Usage**: Specialized software for managing DTF printer output, handling colour profiles, and optimizing prints.
   - **Pros**: Essential for high-quality DTF printing, provides detailed control over print settings and colour management.

Choosing the right file format and software is essential for achieving the best results with DTF printing. For high-quality and scalable designs, vector formats like AI and EPS are ideal. For detailed and transparent images, PNG and TIFF are preferred. The software you choose should match your design needs and workflow, with Adobe products being the industry standard, while open-source alternatives like GIMP and Inkscape offer great functionality without the cost.

Design guidelines for optimal DTF printing.

When preparing files for DTF printing, ensure they are at the appropriate resolution (usually 300 DPI or higher) and have the correct colour profiles set (typically CMYK for print). Using the right RIP software will also be crucial to ensure the best output quality from your DTF printer.

Designing for Direct-to-Film printing involves several key considerations to ensure optimal quality and durability of the prints. Here are detailed design guidelines to follow to achieve the best results:

1. File Preparation and Resolution

- **High Resolution**: Use a resolution of at least 300 DPI (dots per inch). This ensures that your design is sharp and detailed when printed.

- **Vector Graphics**: Whenever possible, use vector graphics (like AI or EPS files) for designs that need to be scalable without loss of quality. This is especially important for logos and text.

- **Raster Images**: If using raster images (like PNG or JPEG), ensure they are high-resolution to avoid pixelation.

2. Color Management

- **Colour Mode**: Set your design to CMYK colour mode. This is crucial because DTF printers typically use CMYK inks, and designing in this mode helps ensure colour accuracy.

- **Colour Profiles**: Use ICC colour profiles provided by the printer manufacturer or your RIP software to ensure accurate colour reproduction.

- **Vibrant Colors**: DTF printing can produce vivid colours, so take advantage of this by designing with bright, bold colours. Avoid relying on subtle colour differences that might not print accurately.

3. Design Elements and Effects

- **Avoid Fine Details**: Fine lines and tiny details may not print well and can get lost or become blurry. Ensure all lines and text are thick enough to be legible.

- **Gradients and Shading**: Use gradients and shading cautiously. While DTF printers handle gradients better than some other methods, ensure they are smooth and not too abrupt to avoid banding.

- **Transparency and Opacity**: DTF printing supports transparency, but it's important to check how these elements print, especially on dark garments. Ensure transparent areas are properly defined.

4. Text and Typography

- **Font Size**: Use a minimum font size of 12 pt for legibility. Smaller text can become unclear when printed.

- **Font Weight**: Use bold or medium-weight fonts. Thin fonts can be difficult to read and might not print cleanly.

- **Outlining Text**: Convert text to outlines (vectorize) to avoid font issues and ensure that the text prints exactly as designed.

5. File Layers and Layout

- **Flattened Files**: For the final print file, ensure layers are flattened to avoid issues during the printing process. However, keep a layered version for edits.

- **Bleed and Margins**: Include a bleed area (typically 1/8 inch) around your design if it's meant to reach the edges of the print area. This prevents white borders from appearing.

- **Alignment and Positioning**: Ensure that all elements are aligned and positioned correctly. Use guides and grids to keep your design well-organized.

6. White Ink and Underbase

- **White Underbase**: DTF printing often requires a white under base, especially for printing on dark fabrics. Ensure your design includes or accommodates this underbase.

- **White Details**: If your design includes white areas, ensure they are well-defined and account for the white ink layer in the printing process.

7. Background and Borders

- **Transparent Backgrounds**: Use transparent backgrounds for designs that should blend seamlessly into the garment. Ensure no unintended pixels are left in the transparent areas.

- **Avoid Unnecessary Borders**: Avoid using borders around the design unless absolutely necessary, as they can highlight any slight misalignments.

8. Special Effects and Textures

- **Textures**: Consider the texture of the print and the fabric. Fine textures can add depth to your design but might not print as expected.

- **Special Effects**: DTF printing can handle some special effects like metallic or glitter inks. Check with your printer for capabilities and adjust your design to include these effects if desired.

9. Testing and Proofing

- **Print Proofs**: Always print a proof of your design on a similar fabric before doing a full run. This allows you to catch any issues with colour, detail, or alignment.

- **Test Different Fabrics**: Test your design on the actual type of fabric you plan to use. Different fabrics can affect how colours and details appear.

10. Post-Processing Considerations

- **Heat Press Settings**: Ensure your design considers the heat press settings required for DTF transfers, such as temperature, pressure, and time, which can affect the final output.

- **Peel Type**: Be aware of whether your DTF film requires a hot or cold peel and design accordingly. Some designs might be better suited to one type of peel over the other.

Printing Process

Loading and aligning film in the printer.

Properly loading and aligning the film in a DTF printer is vital for achieving high-quality prints and avoiding issues like misalignment, smudging, or jamming. Here's a detailed guide to help you load and align the film correctly.

1. Preparation Before Loading the Film

- **Check Printer Manual**: Always refer to your DTF printer's user manual for specific instructions on loading film as each model may have slight differences.

- **Clean the Printer**: Ensure the printer's film-feeding path is clean and free from dust or debris to prevent film contamination.

- **Check the Film**: Inspect the film for any defects, dirt, or dust. Use a lint-free cloth to wipe it gently if necessary.

- **Correct Side Up** Ensure you are loading the film with the printable side facing up. The printable side usually has a smoother or shinier finish, while the non-printable side may have a matte finish.

2. Loading the Film Roll or Sheet

For Roll-Based DTF Printers:

1. **Place the Roll**: Mount the film roll on the printer's roll holders. Make sure it's securely positioned and the roll is not too tight or too loose.

2. **Feed the Film**: Guide the leading edge of the film into the film feeding path. Many printers have a feed guide or rollers to assist with this.

3. **Align the Edges**: Align the edges of the film with the sides of the feeding path. This ensures the film feeds straight through the printer. Use the alignment guides or markers on your printer if available.

4. **Advance the Film**: Use the printer's control panel or manual feed button to advance the film through the feed rollers until it is properly aligned and ready for printing.

5. **Check Tension**: Adjust the tension of the roll to ensure the film feeds smoothly without sagging or pulling too tight.

For Sheet-Based DTF Printers:

1. **Prepare the Sheet**: Ensure the film sheet is cut to the correct size and has clean, straight edges.

2. **Insert the Sheet**: Place the sheet on the printer's input tray or manual feed slot. Align the sheet with the alignment guides on the tray to ensure it feeds straight.

3. **Adjust the Guides**: Move the side guides of the input tray to fit snugly against the edges of the film sheet. This helps maintain proper alignment during printing.

3. Alignment and Calibration

1. **Initial Feed Check**: Once the film is loaded, use the printer's control panel to feed a small portion of the film forward. Check to ensure it feeds evenly and does not skew to one side.

2. **Print a Test Alignment**: Many DTF printers have a test print or alignment function. Use this to print an alignment test pattern and ensure the film is correctly positioned.

3. **Manual Adjustments**: If the alignment is off, use the manual adjustment knobs or levers on your printer to fine-tune the position of the film.

4. **Auto-Align Features**: Some printers come with automatic alignment features. If available, enable these settings to assist with film alignment.

4. Monitoring During Printing

1. **Watch the Feed**: Keep an eye on the film as it feeds through the printer during the first few prints. Look for any signs of misalignment or feeding issues.

2. **Check for Jams**: Be alert for any jams or stoppages. If a jam occurs, stop the printer immediately and carefully remove the film to prevent damage.

3. **Observe Print Quality**: Monitor the print quality for any signs of misalignment or skewing, which may indicate the film is not feeding correctly.

5. Post-Printing Handling

1. **Cut the Film**: If using roll film, cut the printed portion off the roll with clean, straight cuts. Use a sharp blade or scissors to avoid jagged edges.

2. **Inspect the Print**: Check the printed film for alignment and quality. Ensure the print is centred and not skewed.

3. **Store Remaining Film**: Store unused film properly to prevent dust or damage. Keep it rolled neatly and protected in a dust-free environment.

Tips for Success

- **Regular Maintenance**: Keep your printer's feed rollers and paths clean and well-maintained to ensure smooth film feeding.

- **Use High-Quality Film**: Ensure you use good quality DTF film compatible with your printer to avoid feeding and alignment issues.

- **Consistent Environment**: Work in a consistent temperature and humidity environment to minimize the film's physical changes that could affect alignment.

- **Training and Practice**: Regular practice and familiarity with your DTF printer's loading mechanism will make the process smoother and quicker over time.

Selecting print settings and profiles.

Selecting the right print settings and profiles is essential for achieving high-quality and accurate results in Direct-to-Film (DTF) printing. This involves configuring various aspects of your printer, RIP software, and colour management to match your specific print job requirements. Here's a comprehensive guide to help you select the optimal print settings and profiles for DTF printing:

1. Printer and RIP Software Configuration

Printer Settings

- **Printer Model**: Ensure that the printer model is correctly selected in your RIP software. This ensures compatibility and access to the correct settings.

- **Media Type**: Select the appropriate media type for DTF film. Some printers have specific settings for film, which can optimize ink deposition and drying.

- **Resolution**: Set the print resolution to match the requirements of your design. Higher resolutions (e.g., 1440x1440 DPI) yield better detail but may increase print time and ink usage.

RIP Software Settings

- **RIP Software**: Use dedicated RIP software compatible with your DTF printer. Examples include AcroRip, EK Print Studio, and Kothari PrintPro. These tools provide advanced control over colour management, layout, and print parameters.

- **Print Mode**: Choose the print mode based on your design's complexity and the desired quality. Common modes include:

  o **High Quality**: For detailed and high-resolution prints.

  o **Standard**: Balanced setting for general use.

  o **Draft**: Faster printing with lower ink usage, suitable for preliminary tests.

- **Print Speed**: Adjust the print speed based on the desired balance between quality and productivity. Slower speeds generally yield higher quality.

2. Color Management and Profiles

Colour Mode and Profiles

- **Colour Mode**: Ensure your design is in CMYK colour mode. Most DTF printers use CMYK inks, and working in this mode helps maintain colour accuracy from screen to print.

- **ICC Profiles**: Use ICC colour profiles specific to your printer, ink, and film combination. These profiles help translate the colours in your design to what can be accurately reproduced by the printer.

  o **Loading ICC Profiles**: Install and select the ICC profiles provided by your printer or ink manufacturer in your RIP software.

- o **Custom Profiles**: For critical colour accuracy, consider creating custom ICC profiles using a colour calibration device.

Ink Configuration

- **White Ink Layer**: Configure the white ink layer (under base) settings. This layer is crucial for ensuring colours appear vibrant on dark or coloured fabrics.

  - o **Underbase Options**: Adjust the amount and positioning of the white underbase. Some designs may need a heavier underbase for more opacity, while others may require less.

  - o **Spot Color**: Use the spot colour settings in your RIP software to fine-tune the white ink application, especially if the design includes specific white elements.

3. File Preparation and Layout

Design Setup

- **Bleed and Margins**: Ensure your design includes bleed if necessary and that important elements are within the safe print area to avoid being cut off.

- **Alignment**: Check that the design is centred and properly aligned on the film. Use guides and grids in your design software to help with this.

Film and Layout Settings

- **Film Size**: Set the correct film size in the print settings to match your media. Incorrect sizing can lead to misalignment or cut-off prints.

- **Multiple Prints**: If printing multiple designs on the same film, ensure they are properly spaced to avoid overlap and facilitate cutting after printing.

4. Advanced Print Settings

- **Halftone Settings**: Adjust halftone settings to control how gradients and shading are printed. This can help avoid banding and improve the smoothness of colour transitions.

- **Dithering**: Choose an appropriate dithering method to improve the appearance of colour gradients and fine details. Options typically include error diffusion and pattern-based dithering.

Ink Density and Drying

- **Ink Density**: Set the ink density levels in your RIP software. Higher density can enhance colour vibrancy but may require longer drying times.

- **Drying Settings**: Adjust the drying time and temperature settings based on your printer and ink. Proper drying prevents smudging and ensures adhesion to the film.

5. Test Prints and Adjustments

- **Print Proofs**: Always perform test prints on a small section of the film or similar material before committing to a full run. This helps verify that all settings are correct.

- **Adjustments**: Based on the test prints, make any necessary adjustments to the colour profiles, ink density, or print speed to achieve the desired quality.

- **Calibration**: Periodically calibrate your printer and RIP software to maintain consistent print quality. This includes checking and adjusting colour profiles and alignment.

6. Final Checks and Printing

- **Review Settings**: Double-check all settings before starting the print job. Ensure that the correct profiles, media type, and print mode are selected.

- **Monitor the Print**: Keep an eye on the first few prints to ensure everything is working as expected. Look for any signs of misalignment, colour issues, or feeding problems.

- **Post-Print Handling**: Handle printed film carefully to avoid smudging or damage. Follow your printer's guidelines for curing and finishing the printed film.

Monitoring print progress and quality checks.

Monitoring print progress and conducting quality checks are good for successful DTF printing, especially to ensure high-quality output and to catch any issues early. Here's what you need to do:

1. Pre-Print Setup and Checks

Calibration and Test Prints

- **Printer Calibration**: Regularly calibrate your printer to maintain colour accuracy and alignment. Use calibration tools provided by the printer manufacturer or the RIP software.

- **Nozzle Check**: Perform a nozzle check before starting a print job to ensure all print heads are functioning correctly and there are no clogs.

- **Alignment Test**: Run alignment tests to ensure that the print heads are correctly aligned. This is crucial for maintaining print quality, especially for detailed designs.

- **Test Print**: Print a small test section of your design to check for colour accuracy, resolution, and any potential issues with the film or ink application.

2. During the Print Job

Real-Time Monitoring

- **Software Interface**: Use your RIP software's interface to monitor the print job. This can show real-time progress, remaining time, and alerts for any issues.

- **On-Screen Preview**: Many RIPs provide a preview of the print. Ensure that the preview matches your expectations and there are no unexpected changes.

- **Progress Indicators**: Watch for progress bars or indicators on your printer or software to gauge how much of the job is complete and the estimated time remaining.

- **Visual Inspection**: Regularly check the print head and film feed during printing. Look for signs of misalignment, ink smudging, or feeding issues.

- **Check for Smudging**: Watch for any ink smudging, especially when printing dense areas of colour. Adjust the drying settings or ink density if needed.

- **Film Tension and Feed**: Ensure the film is feeding smoothly without any wrinkles or misalignment. Adjust the film tension and alignment if necessary.

Environment Control

- **Temperature and Humidity**: Maintain a consistent environment in your printing area. Extreme changes in temperature or humidity can affect print quality and film handling.

- **Dust and Debris**: Keep the printing area clean to prevent dust and debris from contaminating the film or print heads.

3. Post-Print Quality Checks

Immediate Inspection

- **Colour and Detail**: Check the printed film immediately for colour accuracy, sharpness, and detail. Compare it against your design and test prints.

- **Alignment**: Ensure that the print is properly aligned on the film and that there are no shifts or distortions.

- **Ink Coverage**: Inspect the ink coverage to ensure it is even and consistent. Look for any gaps, streaks, or over-saturation.

Drying and Handling

- **Drying Time**: Allow sufficient drying time for the ink. Depending on the printer and ink type, this can vary. Ensure that the print is fully dry before handling.

- **Post-Drying Inspection**: Once dried, inspect the print again for any changes in colour or detail. Sometimes issues can become more apparent after drying.

Curing Process

- **Heat Press Settings**: Follow the recommended heat press settings for DTF transfers, including temperature, pressure, and time.

- **Peel Test**: After curing, perform a peel test to ensure the transfer adheres well to the garment and there is no peeling or lifting.

- **Final Inspection**: Inspect the transferred design on the garment. Check for any imperfections, incomplete transfers, or colour discrepancies.

4. Common Issues and Troubleshooting

Ink and Color Issues

- **Banding**: Horizontal or vertical lines appearing in the print. This can be caused by misaligned print heads or inconsistent ink flow. Perform print head alignment and cleaning.

- **Color Shifts**: Colors appear differently than expected. Check your colour profiles and calibration settings.

- **Over-Saturation**: Excessive ink causing smudging or bleeding. Adjust the ink density and ensure proper drying time.

Mechanical and Feeding Problems

- **Film Skewing**: Film feeding unevenly or skewing during the print. Check the film alignment and tension.

- **Paper Jams**: Film getting stuck or jamming in the printer. Ensure the film is loaded correctly and there are no obstructions.

- **Print Head Clogs**: Ink not being applied evenly or missing areas. Perform a nozzle check and cleaning routine.

5. Documenting and Adjusting

- **Record Settings**: Keep detailed records of the settings used for each print job, including resolution, ink density, and RIP configurations. This helps in replicating successful prints and troubleshooting issues.

- **Photo Documentation**: Take photos of successful prints and any issues for reference. This can help in diagnosing problems and improving future print jobs.

Making Adjustments

- **Fine-Tune Settings**: Based on the results and inspections, adjust the print settings in your RIP software. This might include changing the resolution, colour profiles, or ink density.

- **Repeat Test Prints**: If adjustments are made, perform additional test prints to validate the changes and ensure consistent quality.

Post-Printing Steps

Curing and powder application.

In Direct-to-Film printing, the application of adhesive powder and the curing process are crucial steps that determine the adhesion, durability, and overall quality of the transfer. These are how to properly apply adhesive powder and cure the print:

1. Adhesive Powder Application

Adhesive powder enables the ink to adhere to the fabric during the heat transfer. Proper application ensures the transfer is durable and has a strong bond with the fabric.

Types of Adhesive Powder

1. **Standard Powder**: Made from thermoplastic polyurethane (TPU), this powder is suitable for most fabric types and provides a strong bond and soft feel.

2. **Low-Temperature Powder**: Designed for sensitive fabrics that cannot withstand high heat, such as synthetic materials.

3. **Speciality Powders**: These may include powders that provide specific finishes like matte or glossy effects or powders formulated for specific types of fabrics.

Powder Application Process

1. **Prepare the Film**

   - Ensure the printed film is clean and the ink is wet. Powder should be applied immediately after printing to ensure it sticks properly to the wet ink.

2. **Applying the Powder**

   - **Manual Application**: For small batches or individual prints:

     - Place the film on a flat, clean surface.

     - Using a powder shaker or a spoon, sprinkle the adhesive powder over the entire printed area. Ensure the powder covers all inked parts uniformly.

     - Hold the film at an angle and gently tap it to allow excess powder to slide off, ensuring an even coating.

   - **Automated Application**: For larger batches or production settings:

     - Use an automated powder application machine. These machines evenly distribute the powder across the print and remove excess powder automatically.

     - Set the machine to the appropriate settings for your powder type and print size.

3. **Removing Excess Powder**

   - After the powder has been applied, gently shake or tap the film to remove any excess powder. Ensure that only the inked areas retain the powder.
   - Use a soft brush or a clean cloth to lightly brush off excess powder from non-printed areas.

4. **Ensuring Even Coverage**

- Inspect the film to ensure there are no areas with excess powder or spots that are missing powder.
- Adjust the powdering process as needed to achieve a smooth, even layer.

Curing Methods

1. **Oven Curing**

   - **Preheat the Oven**: Set the oven to the recommended temperature, usually between 100°C to 150°C (212°F to 302°F), depending on the powder type.
   - **Place the Film**: Place the powdered film in the oven on a flat tray or rack.
   - **Cure Time**: Typically, curing takes about 2-5 minutes. The powder should melt and form a smooth, glossy layer without bubbling.
   - **Check the Curing**: Monitor the film closely to avoid over-curing or burning. The powder should be completely melted and evenly distributed.

2. **Heat Press Curing**

   - **Preheat the Heat Press**: Set the heat press to the recommended temperature for the powder type, usually around 150°C to 170°C (302°F to 338°F).
   - **Use a Hovering Technique**: Instead of pressing down, hover the heat press plate about 1 inch above the film for 2-3 minutes. This will melt the powder without flattening the print.
   - **Check the Film**: Ensure the powder has melted and bonded to the ink. Avoid direct contact to prevent squashing the powder into the ink.

3. **Flash Curing**

   - **Setup**: Use a flash cure unit, commonly used in screen printing.
   - **Preheat**: Set the unit to around 150°C to 160°C (302°F to 320°F).
   - **Cure Time**: Flash-cure the film for 10-15 seconds until the powder melts into a clear, glossy layer.

1. **Inspect the Film**

    -   After curing, check the film for even and complete melting of the powder.
    -   The powder should form a smooth and uniform layer over the inked areas.

2. **Cooling**

    -   Allow the cured film to cool down completely before handling or cutting. This prevents smudging or distorting the print.

3. **Handling**

    -   Handle the film carefully to avoid touching the inked areas. Use clean hands or gloves to prevent fingerprints and dust contamination.

3. Common Issues and Troubleshooting

1. **Uneven Powder Distribution**

    -   **Cause**: Uneven application or excess powder not properly removed.
    -   **Solution**: Ensure consistent powder application and thorough removal of excess powder.

2. **Powder Not Melting Properly**

    -   **Cause**: Incorrect curing temperature or time.
    -   **Solution**: Adjust the curing temperature or time to ensure proper melting. Verify with the powder manufacturer's recommendations.

3. **Over-Curing**

    -   **Cause**: Excessive heat or curing time causing the powder to burn or discolor.
    -   **Solution**: Reduce the curing temperature or duration. Monitor closely during the curing process.

4. **Poor Adhesion to Fabric**

- **Cause**: Insufficient powder or improper curing.
- **Solution**: Ensure an adequate layer of powder is applied and properly melted. Adjust curing settings as necessary.

Heat pressing and transferring designs to the final substrate.

Transferring designs from DTF prints to the final substrate, such as fabric, involves a critical heat-pressing process. This process ensures the design adheres firmly to the substrate and provides a durable and high-quality finish. Here's a detailed guide:

1. Preparation Before Heat Pressing

Tools and Materials Needed

- **DTF Printed Film**: Ensure your DTF film with the cured design is ready for transfer.

- **Heat Press Machine**: A reliable heat press machine with adjustable temperature, pressure, and time settings.

- **Final Substrate**: The fabric or material you are transferring the design to. Common substrates include cotton, polyester, blends, and even some non-fabric materials.

- **Heat-Resistant Tape**: To hold the film in place on the substrate.

- **Parchment Paper or Teflon Sheet**: Place between the heat press plate and the film to prevent sticking and protect the design.

- **Lint Roller**: To clean the substrate surface before pressing.

- **Heat-Resistant Gloves**: For safety while handling hot materials.

Preparing the Substrate

- **Clean the Surface**: Use a lint roller or brush to remove any dust, lint, or fibres from the surface of the fabric. This ensures a smooth and clean transfer.

- **Pre-Pressing**: Pre-press the substrate for a few seconds to remove moisture and wrinkles. This also helps in better adhesion of the transfer.

2. Aligning the DTF Film

Positioning the Design

- **Centre the Design**: Place the DTF film on the substrate in the desired position. Ensure it is centred and aligned properly.

- **Secure with Tape**: Use heat-resistant tape to hold the film in place, especially if the design is large or complex. This prevents shifting during the pressing process.

3. Heat Pressing the Design

Heat Press Settings

- **Temperature**: Set the heat press to the recommended temperature for your adhesive powder and substrate. Typically, this ranges from 150°C to 180°C (302°F to 356°F).

- **Pressure**: Adjust the pressure according to the substrate and the complexity of the design. Medium to firm pressure is often suitable for most fabrics.

- **Time**: Set the pressing time to about 15-20 seconds. This can vary based on the specific powder and film used, so refer to the manufacturer's guidelines.

Pressing the Design

1. **Cover with Parchment Paper/Teflon Sheet**: Place a piece of parchment paper or a Teflon sheet over the film to protect the design and the heat press plate.

2. **Lower the Heat Press**: Carefully lower the heat press onto the substrate with the film.

3. **Pressing**: Apply consistent pressure for the set time. Avoid lifting the press prematurely to ensure the design adheres properly.

4. **Cooling**: After the time is up, lift the heat press and allow the film to cool down slightly (warm peel) or completely (cold peel), depending on the transfer method and powder used.

- **Peel Type**: Check whether your film and powder combination requires a warm or cold peel.

- **Warm Peel**: Peel the film while it is still warm. This method is faster and often used for quicker production cycles.

- **Cold Peel**: Allow the film to cool down completely before peeling. This usually provides a more secure bond and can improve durability.

- **Peeling Technique**: Start peeling from one corner and pull gently at a consistent angle. Ensure that the design adheres to the substrate and no parts lift off with the film.

4. Post-Pressing Finishing

Second Press (Optional)

- **Second Press**: For extra durability, you can perform a second press with parchment paper or a Teflon sheet over the design for about 10 seconds. This helps to secure the transfer further into the fabric.

- **Pressure and Time**: Use the same temperature but reduce the pressing time to avoid overheating.

Inspection and Quality Check

- **Inspect the Transfer**: Check the transferred design for any areas that didn't adhere properly or any imperfections.

- **Feel the Fabric**: Ensure the design feels integrated into the fabric and not just sitting on top.

5. Common Issues and Troubleshooting

Adhesion Problems

- **Poor Adhesion**: If parts of the design don't stick to the fabric, ensure you are using the correct temperature, pressure, and time settings. Check for even powder application.

- **Lifting Edges**: If the edges of the design lift, try increasing the pressure or slightly adjusting the temperature and pressing time.

- **Colour Fading**: Ensure the heat press temperature is not too high as this can cause the colours to fade. Adjust the settings according to the substrate's heat tolerance.

- **Design Distortion**: This can occur if the film shifts during pressing. Secure the film properly and check for even pressure application.

6. Maintenance and Best Practices

Heat Press Maintenance

- **Regular Cleaning**: Clean the heat press platen regularly to remove any adhesive residue or ink buildup.

- **Check Calibration**: Periodically check the calibration of the temperature and pressure settings to ensure they are accurate.

General Tips

- **Consistency**: Always use consistent settings for similar types of transfers to maintain quality.

- **Safety**: Use heat-resistant gloves when handling hot materials and follow all safety guidelines for operating the heat press.

Cooling and finishing processes.

Cooling and finishing processes are the final steps in the Direct-to-Film (DTF) printing workflow, essential for ensuring the longevity and quality of the transferred design. Proper handling during these stages prevents damage and enhances the durability of the print. Here's a comprehensive guide to cooling and finishing your DTF prints:

1. Cooling the Transfer

Immediate Post-Press Handling

- **Lift the Heat Press Carefully**: After the pressing cycle, lift the heat press plate carefully to avoid disturbing the transfer. Use heat-resistant gloves if needed.

- **Allow Time for Cooling**: Depending on the type of peel method (warm or cold peel), allow the appropriate cooling time. This is crucial for the adhesive to set properly.

1. **Warm Peel**:

   - **Peel While Warm**: Gently peel the transfer film while it's still warm to the touch. This method can save time but requires careful handling to avoid smudging or lifting.
   - **Check for Adhesion**: As you peel, ensure the design adheres properly to the fabric. If any part doesn't stick, you may need to press it again with adjusted settings.

2. **Cold Peel**:

   - **Full Cooling**: Let the film cool completely before peeling. This can take several minutes depending on the environment and material thickness.
   - **Enhanced Durability**: Cold peel typically provides a stronger bond and can be less prone to lifting issues.

- **Start from a Corner**: Begin peeling from one corner of the film and slowly pull at a consistent angle.
- **Gentle and Steady**: Pull gently and steadily to avoid tearing the film or lifting parts of the design.
- **Monitor the Transfer**: As you peel, check that all parts of the design remain adhered to the substrate. If any section lifts, pause and re-press if necessary.

2. Post-Peel Finishing

1. **Purpose of Second Press**:

   - **Securing the Design**: A second press helps to further embed the design into the fabric, enhancing durability and ensuring a smooth, finished look.

- **Improving Texture**: It can also smooth out any uneven surfaces and make the print feel more integrated with the fabric.

2. **How to Perform a Second Press**:

- **Cover with Parchment or Teflon**: Place parchment paper or a Teflon sheet over the design to protect it.
- **Adjust Settings**: Use a lower temperature (around 150°C to 160°C) and a shorter pressing time (5-10 seconds) to avoid overheating.
- **Apply Medium Pressure**: Press with medium pressure to ensure even heat distribution without flattening the design excessively.

Edge Check and Re-Pressing

- **Inspect the Edges**: Check the edges and any intricate parts of the design for proper adhesion. If any area seems loose or lifted, re-press that section.
- **Spot Treatment**: For small areas that need re-pressing, use a small piece of Teflon or parchment to focus the heat and pressure on that spot.

3. Final Cooling and Handling

Cooling Down

- **Allow Time to Cool**: Let the garment cool completely before further handling. This helps the adhesive fully set and prevents deformation of the print.
- **Avoid Immediate Washing**: Wait at least 24 hours before washing the garment to allow the adhesive to cure fully.

Inspecting the Finished Product

- **Visual Inspection**: Check the entire design for any defects, lifting, or colour issues.
- **Feel the Fabric**: Ensure the design is smoothly integrated into the fabric without a noticeable ridge or rough texture.
- **Flexibility and Durability**: Gently stretch and flex the fabric to confirm the design's adherence and elasticity.

4. Common Finishing Issues and Troubleshooting

- **Cause**: Insufficient pressure, improper powder application, or uneven heat distribution.
- **Solution**: Increase pressure during the press, ensure even powder coverage, and use a second pressing to secure edges.

Cracking or Peeling

- **Cause**: Overheating, undercured powder, or excessive film movement during pressing.
- **Solution**: Adjust pressing temperature and time, ensure the powder is fully melted and cured, and secure the film to prevent shifting.

Colour Fading or Bleeding

- **Cause**: Excessive heat or incompatible substrate.
- **Solution**: Lower the pressing temperature, check substrate compatibility, and ensure proper pre-treatment of the fabric.

5. Maintenance and Care for DTF Transfers

Garment Care Instructions

- **Washing Guidelines**: Recommend washing the garment inside out in cold water with mild detergent. Avoid bleach and fabric softeners.
- **Drying Instructions**: Air dry or tumble dry on low heat. High heat can weaken the adhesive and damage the print.
- **Ironing Precautions**: If ironing is necessary, place a cloth or parchment paper over the design to protect it. Avoid direct heat on the print.

Long-Term Durability Tips

- **Avoid Harsh Treatments**: Advice against harsh treatments such as dry cleaning or aggressive scrubbing.
- **Proper Storage**: Store the garments in a cool, dry place to prevent moisture or heat damage.
- **Regular Inspections**: Periodically check the durability of the prints, especially for garments used frequently or subjected to heavy wear.

Maintenance and Troubleshooting

Routine Maintenance

Cleaning the printer (print heads, film rollers, etc.).

Regular cleaning and maintenance of a DTF printer are essential to ensure consistent print quality and prolong the life of the printer. Key components such as the print heads, film rollers, and other parts can accumulate ink residue and debris over time, leading to clogs, misalignments, and other issues. Here's a detailed guide.

1. Cleaning the Print Heads

The print heads are critical to achieving high-quality prints, and they require regular maintenance to prevent clogging and ensure smooth ink flow.

Daily Maintenance

1. **Perform Nozzle Checks**:

    - Run a nozzle check from your printer's maintenance menu to ensure all nozzles are firing correctly. This helps identify any blockages early.
    - If you notice missing lines or gaps in the nozzle check pattern, proceed with a cleaning cycle.

2. **Print Head Cleaning Cycle**:

    - Use the printer's built-in cleaning function to clear minor clogs. This process forces ink through the nozzles to clean out any blockages.
    - Follow the printer manufacturer's instructions on how to perform this operation. Usually, this can be done through the printer's control panel or software interface.

3. **Wipe the Print Heads**:

    - If the automatic cleaning doesn't resolve the issue, you may need to manually clean the print heads.
    - Power off the printer and gently move the print head to the maintenance position (if it's not self-locating).

- Use a lint-free cloth or a dedicated cleaning swab lightly moistened with a print head cleaning solution. Wipe the print heads gently to remove any ink residue.

Weekly Maintenance

1. **Deep Cleaning Cycle**:

   - Perform a deep cleaning cycle once a week to thoroughly clean the print heads. This is more intensive than the regular cleaning cycle and helps clear stubborn clogs.
   - Be cautious as excessive use of deep cleaning can waste ink and may affect the print heads over time.

2. **Cap Station and Wiper Blade Cleaning**:

   - Clean the cap station (where the print head rests) and the wiper blade to remove any ink buildup that could transfer back onto the print heads.
   - Use a lint-free cloth or a cotton swab with a cleaning solution to clean these areas.

2. Cleaning the Film Rollers

Film rollers play a vital role in feeding the film smoothly through the printer. Keeping them clean ensures accurate and consistent feeding without slippage or jamming.

Routine Cleaning

1. **Inspect the Rollers**:

   - Regularly inspect the film rollers for any ink smudges, dust, or debris.
   - Check for wear or damage that might affect their performance.

2. **Clean with Lint-Free Cloth**:

   - Turn off the printer and gently wipe the rollers with a lint-free cloth dampened with water or a mild cleaning solution.
   - Rotate the rollers manually to ensure you clean their entire surface.

3. **Avoid Harsh Chemicals**:

- Do not use harsh chemicals or abrasive materials to clean the rollers as they can damage the surface and affect their grip on the film.

3. Cleaning the Print Bed and Surrounding Areas

The print bed and surrounding areas should be kept clean to avoid contaminating the film and print heads.

Regular Cleaning

- **Wipe the Print Bed**: Use a soft, lint-free cloth to wipe the print bed and remove any dust, ink residue, or debris. This helps in maintaining a smooth surface for the film to rest on.
- **Check for Adhesive Residue**: If you use tape or adhesive strips to hold the film in place, remove any residue left on the print bed after each print job. Use a gentle adhesive remover if necessary.
- **Clean the Surrounding Areas**: Dust and clean the areas around the print bed and film feed path. Keeping these areas clean helps prevent debris from being dragged onto the print bed or into the print mechanism.

4. Maintaining the Ink System

Proper maintenance of the ink system ensures consistent ink flow and prevents clogs and colour inconsistencies.

Ink Cartridge and Tank Maintenance

1. **Check Ink Levels**:

   - Regularly monitor ink levels to avoid running the printer on low ink, which can introduce air bubbles into the system and cause clogging.
   - Refill or replace cartridges or ink tanks as needed.

2. **Shake Ink Cartridges**:

   - Gently shake the ink cartridges or bottles (if applicable) periodically to prevent ink sedimentation, especially if the printer has been idle for a while.

3. **Clean Ink Lines**:

- If your printer has refillable ink tanks with lines, ensure they are free of air bubbles and blockages. Perform a system flush or clean the lines according to the manufacturer's instructions.

5. Software and Firmware Maintenance

Keeping your printer's software and firmware updated is crucial for optimal performance and access to new features and fixes.

1. **Firmware Updates**:

   - Check regularly for firmware updates from your printer's manufacturer. These updates can improve performance, fix bugs, and sometimes add new functionalities.
   - Follow the manufacturer's instructions to update the firmware safely.

2. **RIP Software Maintenance**:

   - Ensure your RIP (Raster Image Processor) software is up to date. Software updates often include enhancements and bug fixes that improve print quality and efficiency.
   - Regularly back up your RIP settings and profiles to avoid losing custom configurations during updates.

6. General Maintenance Tips

1. **Daily Start-Up and Shut-Down Routines**:

   - Follow the manufacturer's guidelines for starting up and shutting down the printer. This can include running specific maintenance routines that prime the print heads and check system readiness.

2. **Environment Control**:

   - Keep the printing environment clean and free of dust. Use air purifiers or dust covers when the printer is not in use to protect it from airborne particles.
   - Maintain a stable temperature and humidity level to prevent ink from drying out prematurely or condensation from forming inside the printer.

3. **Regular Professional Maintenance**:

- Schedule periodic professional maintenance with a certified technician, especially for complex or high-end printers. They can perform more thorough checks and service tasks that might be beyond routine user maintenance.

Daily Maintenance Checks

Nozzle and Print Head Health

1. **Perform a Nozzle Check**:

   - Run a nozzle check every day before starting your printing tasks. This will help you identify any clogs or misfiring nozzles early on.
   - Check for missing lines or inconsistent patterns which indicate a need for cleaning.

2. **Clean the Print Heads**:

   - Use the printer's automatic cleaning function if the nozzle check reveals any issues. This routine cleaning helps maintain smooth ink flow and prevents clogs.
   - For stubborn clogs, perform a manual cleaning with a lint-free cloth and appropriate cleaning solution, following the manufacturer's instructions.

Print Bed and Rollers

1. **Inspect and Clean the Print Bed**:

   - Wipe the print bed with a lint-free cloth to remove dust, debris, or any ink residue. This ensures the film lays flat and feeds smoothly during printing.
   - Check for adhesive residue or film fragments and clean them off.

2. **Check and Clean Rollers**:

   - Inspect the film rollers for ink smudges or debris. Clean them with a damp lint-free cloth to maintain their grip and prevent film-feeding issues.

Weekly Maintenance Checks

1. **Monitor Ink Levels**:

   - Check the ink levels to ensure they are sufficient for upcoming print jobs. Refill or replace cartridges as needed to avoid air bubbles or running out of ink mid-print.
   - Gently shake ink cartridges or bottles (if applicable) to prevent sedimentation, especially if the printer has been idle.

2. **Inspect Ink Lines and Dampers**:

   - If your printer has an ink tank system, check the ink lines and dampers for air bubbles or blockages. Perform a purge or clean the lines as needed to ensure smooth ink flow.

3. **Flush the Ink System**:

   - Perform a system flush using the printer's maintenance settings to clear any built-up ink or debris in the lines and print heads. This can help maintain optimal ink flow and prevent clogging.

General Printer Components

1. **Clean the Cap Station and Wiper Blade**:

   - Use a cotton swab and cleaning solution to clean the cap station (where the print head rests) and the wiper blade. This prevents ink buildup and ensures the print head is properly sealed and cleaned during operation.

2. **Check for Firmware Updates**:

   - Regularly check for and install firmware updates from your printer manufacturer. These updates can improve performance, fix bugs, and sometimes add new features.

3. **Backup RIP Software Settings**:

   - Back up your RIP software settings and profiles regularly. This ensures you can quickly restore your configurations in case of software updates or issues.

Monthly Maintenance Checks

1. **Deep Clean Print Heads**:

   - Perform a deep cleaning cycle to thoroughly clean the print heads and ensure optimal performance. This helps remove any stubborn clogs or dried ink.
   - Be mindful that deep cleaning uses more ink, so balance it with regular maintenance to avoid excessive ink waste.

2. **Inspect Mechanical Parts**:

   - Check the printer's mechanical components, such as belts, gears, and moving parts, for wear or damage. Look for any signs of wear or misalignment that could affect print quality.
   - Lubricate any moving parts as recommended by the manufacturer to ensure smooth operation.

3. **Calibrate Print Head Alignment**:

   - Run a print head alignment calibration to ensure accurate positioning and minimize print distortions or misalignments.
   - Follow the printer's manual for instructions on how to perform this calibration.

Quarterly Maintenance Checks

Comprehensive System Check

1. **Professional Maintenance Service**:

   - Schedule a professional maintenance service with a certified technician. They can perform thorough checks and servicing that go beyond routine maintenance, ensuring all components are in optimal condition.
   - This is particularly important for high-volume or industrial-grade printers.

2. **Replace Worn Parts**:

   - Replace any parts that show significant wear or have reached their recommended lifespan, such as dampers, wipers, or rollers.

- Use genuine replacement parts to maintain compatibility and performance.

3. **Update RIP Software**:

   - Check for and install updates for your RIP software. Updates can include bug fixes, performance improvements, and new features that enhance your printing workflow.

4. **Inspect Electrical Connections**:

   - Inspect the printer's electrical connections and cables for signs of wear, damage, or loose connections. Secure or replace any problematic components to prevent operational issues.

5. Environmental and Usage Considerations

Maintaining a Clean Environment

1. **Control Dust and Debris**:

   - Keep the printer in a clean, dust-free environment. Use air purifiers or covers to minimize dust accumulation when the printer is not in use.
   - Regularly clean the area around the printer to prevent dust and debris from affecting the print quality.

2. **Temperature and Humidity Control**:

   - Maintain a stable temperature and humidity level in the printer's environment. Extreme conditions can affect ink performance and lead to print defects or mechanical issues.
   - Use a dehumidifier or air conditioner if necessary to keep the environment within the recommended range for your printer.

Usage Patterns

1. **Regular Use**:

   - Use the printer regularly to keep the ink flowing and prevent clogs. Infrequent use can lead to dried ink in the nozzles and lines.
   - If the printer will be idle for an extended period, perform a thorough cleaning and follow the manufacturer's instructions for proper storage.

2. **Print Small Test Patterns**:

- Print small test patterns or nozzle checks frequently to keep the print heads in good condition and ensure the system is ready for larger jobs.

Troubleshooting Common Issues

Print Quality Problems

1. **Inconsistent Colors or Banding**:

- Check for clogged nozzles and perform a cleaning cycle if necessary. Ensure proper ink levels and shake cartridges to mix the ink.
- Calibrate the print heads and adjust the print settings in the RIP software to resolve banding issues.

2. **Misaligned Prints**:

- Recalibrate the print head alignment and ensure the film is fed correctly. Inspect and clean the film rollers to prevent feeding issues.
- Verify that the print bed is clean and flat.

Printer Errors and Mechanical Issues

1. **Paper Jams or Film Feeding Problems**:

- Check for any obstructions in the film feed path and ensure the film rollers are clean and free of debris.
- Inspect the film for damage or warping that could cause feeding problems.

2. **Error Messages or Printer Not Responding**:

- Refer to the printer's manual or support resources for troubleshooting steps related to specific error messages.
- Restart the printer and check all connections. Ensure firmware and software are up to date.

Ink and Consumables Management

Replacing ink cartridges and managing ink levels.

Managing ink levels and replacing ink cartridges in your DTF printer ensure continuous and high-quality printing. Proper handling of ink cartridges and monitoring of ink levels can prevent interruptions and maintain the integrity of your prints. Here's a detailed guide.

Remember that DTF printers typically use CMYK (Cyan, Magenta, Yellow, Black) inks, and often white ink for printing on dark fabrics. Effective ink management involves monitoring these ink levels, replacing cartridges or refilling tanks as needed, and maintaining the ink system to avoid issues like air bubbles or clogs.

When to Replace Ink Cartridges

1. **Low Ink Warnings**:

   - Most DTF printers have sensors that alert you when ink levels are low. Pay attention to these warnings to avoid running out of ink during a print job.
   - Plan to replace or refill the ink cartridge soon after receiving the low ink warning.

2. **Poor Print Quality**:

   - Signs like faded colours, streaks, or missing lines in prints can indicate that an ink cartridge is running low or has an air bubble.
   - Regularly inspect the print quality to catch these issues early.

Steps to Replace Ink Cartridges

1. **Prepare New Ink Cartridges**:

   - Ensure you have the correct replacement cartridges for your printer model. Use genuine or recommended cartridges to avoid compatibility issues.
   - Gently shake the new cartridges to mix the ink, especially if they have been sitting for a while.

2. **Access the Ink Cartridges**:

- Power on the printer and open the cover to access the ink cartridges. The printer usually moves the cartridges to an accessible position automatically.
- Follow the manufacturer's instructions to safely open the cartridge compartment.

3. **Remove the Old Cartridge**:

- Carefully release and remove the old cartridge. Be mindful of any ink residue or drips.
- Dispose of the old cartridge according to local regulations or the manufacturer's recycling program.

4. **Install the New Cartridge**:

- Remove any protective seals or caps from the new cartridge.
- Insert the new cartridge into the designated slot, ensuring it clicks into place securely.

5. **Prime the Ink System**:

- After installing the new cartridge, run a print head cleaning cycle or system prime to ensure the new ink flows smoothly.
- Print a test pattern to check that the new cartridge is functioning correctly.

Monitoring Ink Levels

1. **Use Printer Software**:

- Most DTF printers come with software that monitors and displays ink levels. Check these levels regularly through the printer's control panel or associated software.
- Set alerts for low ink levels to prevent unexpected depletion.

2. **Manual Checks**:

- For printers with visible ink tanks, visually inspect the ink levels. Marking the tanks with level indicators can help track usage over time.
- Keep a log of ink consumption to predict when you will need to replace or refill cartridges.

3. **Regular Inspections**:

- Include ink level checks in your routine maintenance schedule. Inspect the ink levels before starting any large or critical print jobs.

1. **Prepare the Refilling Station**:

   - Gather all necessary supplies: compatible ink bottles, gloves, and cleaning materials.
   - Place the printer in a well-ventilated area and protect the surrounding surfaces from potential spills.

2. **Refill the Tanks Carefully**:

   - Open the ink tank cap and slowly pour the ink into the tank, avoiding bubbles and spills. Use a funnel if necessary for precision.
   - Fill the tank to the recommended level without overfilling. Overfilling can cause leaks and affect the printer's performance.

3. **Clean Up**:

   - Wipe any spills immediately and securely close the tank caps to prevent contamination or ink drying.
   - Run a cleaning cycle or prime the ink system to ensure proper ink flow.

Preventing Air Bubbles and Clogs

1. **Regular Usage**:

   - Use the printer regularly to keep the ink flowing and prevent it from drying out in the nozzles. Even printing small test patterns can help.
   - If the printer will be idle for an extended period, perform maintenance tasks recommended by the manufacturer, such as running a system flush or storing the print heads properly.

2. **Avoiding Air Infiltration**:

   - Ensure that ink cartridges and tanks are sealed properly to prevent air from entering the ink system.

- When replacing cartridges or refilling tanks, minimize the exposure of ink lines and nozzles to air.

Regular System Flushing

1. **Scheduled Flushing**:

   - Perform a system flush periodically, especially if using high-viscosity or white inks, which are more prone to settling and clogging.
   - Follow the manufacturer's recommendations for how often to flush the system and the proper procedure to do so.

2. **Check for Blockages**:

   - Inspect the ink lines and dampers for any signs of blockages or ink sediment. Clean or replace them if necessary to maintain smooth ink flow.

Tips for Efficient Ink Usage

1. **Optimize Print Settings**:

   o Use the correct print settings for each job to avoid excessive ink usage. Adjust the resolution and ink density according to the print requirements.

   o Profile your substrates and optimize your RIP software settings to achieve the best balance between print quality and ink usage.

2. **Regular Maintenance**:

   - Perform regular maintenance to keep the printer running efficiently and avoid wasting ink on cleaning cycles or reprints.
   - Keep the printer clean and in good working condition to minimize ink waste.

3. **Store Inks Properly**:

   - Store ink cartridges and bottles in a cool, dry place, away from direct sunlight. Proper storage prevents ink from degrading and ensures it flows correctly when used.

Storing and handling film and other consumables.

Proper storage and handling practices help prevent issues such as film warping, contamination, and premature degradation of inks and powders. Here's a detailed guide on how to store and handle DTF film, inks, powders, and other consumables:

Optimal Storage Conditions

1. **Temperature and Humidity Control**:

   - Store DTF film in a cool, dry place. The ideal storage temperature is between 60-75°F (15-24°C).
   - Maintain relative humidity levels between 40-60%. High humidity can cause the film to absorb moisture and become wavy, while low humidity can make it brittle.

2. **Avoid Direct Sunlight and Heat**:

   - Keep film away from direct sunlight and heat sources. UV light can degrade the film's coating, and excessive heat can warp the film.
   - Store film rolls in their original packaging to protect them from light exposure and dust.

3. **Keep Film Flat or Upright**:

   - For rolled film, store the rolls upright in a vertical position to prevent them from developing flat spots or becoming misshapen.
   - If storing flat sheets, keep them in a flat position, preferably in a storage cabinet or drawer that protects them from bending or creasing.

4. **Protect from Dust and Contaminants**:

   - Store film in a clean, dust-free environment. Use dust covers or store in sealed containers to prevent dust and contaminants from settling on the film surface.
   - Avoid storing film near chemicals or substances with strong odours, as these can affect the film's coating and printability.

1. **Handle with Clean Hands or Gloves**:

   - Always handle DTF film with clean hands or wear cotton gloves to avoid transferring oils, dirt, or fingerprints onto the film surface.
   - Hold the film by its edges and avoid touching the printable side to maintain its pristine condition.

2. **Cut and Trim Carefully**:

   - Use sharp scissors or a rotary cutter to cut and trim the film. Dull blades can cause jagged edges or damage the film's coating.
   - Measure and cut in a clean, dust-free area to prevent contamination.

3. **Minimize Exposure to Air**:

   - When not in use, keep the film in its original packaging or a re-sealable bag to minimize exposure to air and humidity.
   - Roll up any unused film and secure it with a soft band to keep it tightly wound.

Optimal Storage Conditions

1. **Temperature Control**:

   - Store DTF inks in a cool, stable environment. The ideal storage temperature is between 50-77°F (10-25°C).
   - Avoid freezing temperatures or excessive heat, as these can affect the ink's consistency and performance.

2. **Avoid Direct Sunlight**:

   - Keep inks away from direct sunlight and strong UV light. UV exposure can degrade the ink's colour and quality.
   - Store inks in their original, opaque bottles or containers to protect them from light exposure.

3. **Upright Storage**:

   - Store ink bottles upright to prevent leaks and spills.

- Ensure that ink bottles are tightly capped to prevent air exposure and contamination.

1. **Shake Before Use**:

   - Gently shake ink bottles before use to mix the contents thoroughly, especially if the ink has been sitting for a while.
   - Avoid vigorous shaking that can introduce air bubbles into the ink.

2. **Clean Refilling Process**:

   - When refilling ink tanks or cartridges, use a clean funnel or syringe to avoid spills and ensure precise filling.
   - Perform refilling in a clean area to prevent contaminants from entering the ink system.

3. **Use Fresh Ink**:

   - Use ink within the recommended shelf life specified by the manufacturer. Expired ink can lead to poor print quality and clogging.
   - Rotate your stock to use the oldest inks first (FIFO method).

Storing and Handling DTF Powder Adhesive

Optimal Storage Conditions

1. **Temperature and Humidity Control**:

   - Store DTF powder adhesive in a cool, dry place with a temperature between 60-75°F (15-24°C) and relative humidity of 40-60%.
   - Keep the powder sealed in its original container to prevent it from absorbing moisture from the air.

2. **Avoid Direct Sunlight and Heat**:

   - Keep the powder away from direct sunlight and heat sources. Excessive heat can affect its adhesive properties.
   - Store in a dark, cool area to maintain its effectiveness.

3. **Store in a Sealed Container**:

- After opening, reseal the container tightly to keep the powder fresh and prevent clumping.
- If transferring the powder to another container, use one that is airtight and suitable for powder storage.

Handling DTF Powder Adhesive

1. **Handle with Care**:

- Handle the powder gently to avoid creating dust clouds. Use a scoop or spoon to measure out the required amount.
- Wear gloves and a mask if handling large quantities to avoid skin contact and inhalation of fine particles.

2. **Apply Evenly**:

- Apply the powder evenly over the wet ink on the film. Shake off any excess powder to prevent clumps and ensure a smooth finish.
- Work in a clean area to avoid contaminating the powder or the printed film.

3. **Clean Up Residue**:

- After application, clean up any powder residue from your work area to prevent it from affecting other prints or surfaces.
- Use a vacuum or damp cloth to collect and dispose of loose powder safely.

Substrates and Transfer Sheets

1. **Store in a Clean, Flat Area**:

- Store substrates (e.g., T-shirts, textiles) and transfer sheets flat to prevent wrinkles and creases.
- Keep them in a dust-free environment and away from direct sunlight to avoid discolouration or damage.

2. **Protect from Moisture and Contaminants**:

- Keep substrates in sealed bags or containers to protect them from moisture, dust, and contaminants.

- Use silica gel packets in storage containers to help control moisture levels.

3. **Handle with Clean Hands**:

    - Handle substrates and transfer sheets with clean hands or gloves to prevent transferring oils and dirt.
    - Inspect each item before use to ensure it is free from defects or contaminants.

Fixing alignment and calibration issues.

Alignment and calibration problems can lead to misprints, overlapping images, or skewed designs, affecting the overall output quality. Here's a comprehensive guide on how to diagnose and fix alignment and calibration issues in DTF printing:

1. Identifying Alignment and Calibration Issues

Symptoms of Alignment Problems

1. **Misalignment Between Colors or Layers**:

    - Designs appear offset or misaligned when printing multiple colours or layers.
    - Colours do not line up properly, resulting in blurred or distorted images.

2. **Substrate Feeding Issues**:

    - Substrates or DTF film do not feed straight or consistently through the printer.
    - Prints appear skewed or crooked on the substrate.

3. **Print Head Misalignment**:

    - Lines or patterns in prints appear uneven or skewed, indicating a misalignment of print heads.

Nozzle Check and Test Prints

1. **Perform a Nozzle Check**:

- Print a nozzle check pattern to ensure all print heads are firing correctly and producing consistent lines.
- Identify any missing or misfiring nozzles that could affect alignment and print quality.

2. **Print Alignment Test Patterns**:

- Use built-in alignment test patterns or create test designs with precise alignment markers (e.g., crosshairs, grid lines).
- Print these test patterns to visually assess alignment accuracy across multiple colours and layers.

Calibration and Adjustment Steps

1. **Check Printer Settings and Software**

- **Verify Printer Settings**: Ensure that printer settings such as resolution, media type, and print speed are correctly configured in the RIP software or printer driver.
- **Adjust Print Head Alignment**: Use the printer's alignment adjustment settings to fine-tune the positioning of print heads. This adjustment varies by printer model and may involve manual adjustments or software settings.

2. **Perform Mechanical Checks**

- **Inspect Media Loading Mechanism**: Ensure that the DTF film or substrate is loaded correctly and aligned properly within the printer's media feeding mechanism.
- **Clean and Check Rollers**: Clean film rollers and check for any debris or residue that could affect media feeding and alignment.

3. **Calibrate Print Bed or Platen**

- **Run Print Bed Calibration**: Follow the manufacturer's instructions to calibrate the print bed or platen. This process ensures that the substrate is positioned accurately for printing.
- **Check Substrate Flatness**: Ensure that substrates are flat and smooth before loading them into the printer. Warped or wrinkled substrates can cause alignment issues.

4. **Adjust Print Head Settings**

- **Fine-tune Print Head Alignment**: Use software tools or adjustment settings to align print heads precisely. Some printers allow for manual adjustment of individual print heads to correct alignment discrepancies.

5. **Check and Update Firmware/Software**

- **Update Printer Firmware**: Check for firmware updates from the printer manufacturer. Updates may include improvements to alignment algorithms or printer performance.
- **Update RIP Software**: Ensure that your RIP (Raster Image Processor) software is up to date. Software updates often include enhancements that improve print alignment and accuracy.

Resolving software and connectivity problems.

Software issues can range from compatibility issues with your RIP software or printer drivers to connectivity problems affecting communication between devices.

Common Symptoms

1. **Print Job Errors**:

- Print jobs fail to start or stop midway without completing.
- Error messages related to file processing or print data transmission appear on the computer or printer display.

2. **Software Crashes or Freezes**:

- RIP software or printer driver crashes unexpectedly during operation.
- The software becomes unresponsive when sending print jobs or adjusting settings.

3. **Communication Errors**:

- The printer status shows as offline or disconnected, even when physically connected.
- Inconsistent data transmission between the computer and printer leads to print delays or errors.

1. **Check Software Compatibility**

   - **Verify System Requirements**: Ensure that your computer meets the minimum system requirements for the RIP software and printer drivers.
   - **Update Software**: Check for updates to the RIP software and install the latest version to address compatibility issues with operating system updates or hardware changes.

2. **Review Print Settings and Job Configuration**

   - **Verify Print Settings**: Double-check print settings such as resolution, colour profiles, and media type settings in the RIP software.
   - **Adjust Job Configuration**: Modify print job configurations to optimize settings for the specific substrate and design requirements.

3. **Clear Print Queues and Restart Software**

   - **Clear Print Queues**: Remove any pending print jobs from the print queue to prevent conflicts or errors.
   - **Restart Software**: Close the RIP software and restart it to refresh the software interface and clear temporary glitches.

4. **Check File Integrity and Compatibility**

   - **File Format Compatibility**: Ensure that design files (e.g., PNG, JPEG, PDF) are compatible with the RIP software and printer.
   - **Repair Corrupt Files**: If encountering errors with specific files, attempt to repair or re-save them to ensure data integrity.

Resolving Connectivity Issues

1. **Verify Physical Connections**

   - **Check Cables**: Inspect USB, Ethernet, or Wi-Fi cables for damage or loose connections. Ensure they are securely plugged into the printer and computer.

- **Restart Devices**: Power cycle the printer, computer, and networking equipment (routers or switches) to reset connections.

2. **Network Configuration**

   - **Wi-Fi and Ethernet Settings**: Verify network settings on the printer and ensure it is connected to the correct network.
   - **IP Address Assignment**: Set a static IP address for the printer to prevent dynamic IP conflicts that can disrupt connectivity.

3. **Firewall and Security Settings**

   - **Firewall Permissions**: Adjust firewall settings to allow communication between the computer and printer. Add exceptions for the RIP software or printer drivers if necessary.
   - **Antivirus Software**: Temporarily disable or adjust antivirus settings to prevent interference with print job data transmission.

4. **Update Drivers and Firmware**

   - **Printer Drivers**: Install the latest printer drivers compatible with your operating system. Check the manufacturer's website for updates.
   - **Firmware Updates**: Update the printer's firmware to improve stability, fix bugs, and enhance connectivity features.

Print Test Pages

   - After troubleshooting, print test pages or sample designs to verify that software and connectivity issues have been resolved.
   - Evaluate the print quality and ensure that colours, alignment, and overall output meet expectations.
   - **Perform Advanced Maintenance Tasks** and Replace worn-out components such as belts, gears, or rollers that affect printer performance and alignment.
   - **Lubrication**: Apply lubricants as recommended by the manufacturer to maintain smooth mechanical operation.

Predictive Maintenance Strategies:

   - **Usage Patterns Analysis**: Analyze printer usage patterns and historical data to predict maintenance needs, such as component replacements or preventive maintenance tasks.

- o **Scheduled Maintenance**: Implement scheduled maintenance routines based on printer usage metrics and diagnostic results to prevent downtime and optimize performance.

Advanced Features and Customization

Printer Settings and Custom Profiles

Setting up printer settings and custom profiles in Direct-to-Film printing is essential for achieving accurate colour reproduction, optimizing ink usage, and ensuring consistent print quality across various substrates.

Basic Printer Settings

- **Resolution**: Choose the appropriate resolution based on the desired print quality and substrate type. Higher resolutions (e.g., 1440 dpi) offer finer detail but may require more time and ink.
- **Media Type**: Select the media type setting that matches the DTF film or substrate being used (e.g., glossy, matte, cotton). This setting adjusts ink application and drying times for optimal results.
- **Ink Density**: Adjust ink density to control the amount of ink deposited on the substrate. This setting can impact colour saturation, drying times, and ink consumption.
- **Print Speed**: Balance print speed with print quality requirements. Higher speeds may sacrifice detail and colour accuracy, while slower speeds can enhance print resolution and reduce banding.
- **Drying Time**: Set drying times to allow sufficient ink drying between layers or during multi-pass printing. This prevents smudging and improves colour layering.

Creating Custom Color Profiles

Importance of Color Management

1. **Color Calibration Tools**:

   - Use spectrophotometers or colourimeters to measure colour accuracy and create custom ICC profiles. These tools ensure consistent colour reproduction across different printers, inks, and substrates.

2. **Software for Profiling**:

- Utilize colour profiling software (e.g., X-Rite i1Profiler, ColorMunki) to generate custom ICC profiles based on specific ink and substrate combinations.
- Follow the software's step-by-step instructions to create accurate colour profiles that match your printing environment.

Calibration and Profiling Process

- **Gather Necessary Equipment**: Obtain a spectrophotometer or colourimeter compatible with your printer model and colour profiling software.
- **Prepare the Printing Environment**: Ensure consistent lighting conditions and ambient temperature in the printing environment to minimize colour variation during profiling.

Print and Measure Color Patches:

- Print a set of colour patches or target charts provided by the profiling software on your DTF printer.
- Allow the prints to dry completely before proceeding to measurement.
- **Measure Color Data**: Use the spectrophotometer or colourimeter to measure colour data from the printed patches. Follow the software's instructions to capture accurate measurements.
- **Generate ICC Profiles**: Input the colour measurement data into the profiling software to generate custom ICC profiles. The software will calculate colour corrections to achieve accurate colour reproduction.

Validate and Install Profiles:

- Validate the generated ICC profiles by printing test images or colour charts to verify colour accuracy and consistency.
- Install the validated profiles in your RIP software or printer driver settings for use in future print jobs.

Integration with RIP Software

1. **Profile Installation**:

- Install the custom ICC profiles in your RIP software or printer driver settings. Refer to the software's user manual for instructions on profile installation.

2. **Profile Selection**:

- Select the appropriate ICC profile in the RIP software when preparing print jobs. Assign profiles based on the specific ink, substrate, and print conditions for each job.

3. **Profile Maintenance**:

- Periodically recalibrate and update ICC profiles to account for changes in ink batches, substrate variations, or environmental factors.
- Store ICC profiles in a secure location and maintain backup copies for future reference or reinstallation.

Using RIP Software for DTF Printing

RIP software enhances the capabilities of DTF printers by providing advanced features for image processing, colour management, and job management. Here's a comprehensive guide on how to effectively utilize RIP software for DTF printing:

Key Functions and Benefits

1. **Colour Management**:

- **ICC Profiles**: RIP software allows you to import and manage custom ICC profiles for precise colour reproduction across different substrates and ink sets.
- **Colour Correction**: Adjust colour balance, saturation, and density to achieve optimal print results.

2. **Image Processing**:

- **Halftoning**: Convert continuous tone images into halftone patterns (e.g., dots, lines) for accurate ink application and smooth gradients.
- **Image Scaling and Positioning**: Resize, rotate, and position images on the print bed for efficient media usage and layout customization.

3. **Workflow Automation**:

- **Job Queues**: Organize and schedule print jobs in queues to optimize production efficiency and manage print order priorities.
- **Batch Processing**: Automate repetitive tasks such as file processing, colour management, and printing to reduce manual intervention.

4. **Media and Substrate Management**:

- **Media Profiles**: Store and apply media-specific settings and profiles for different types of DTF films, fabrics, or other substrates.
- **Media Feed Calibration**: Fine-tune media feeding parameters to ensure accurate substrate placement and print alignment.